THE LITTLE BOOK OF

LEICESTERSHIRE

NATASHA SHELDON

The History Press

To my nans,
Doris, Irene and Lillian,
who helped ignite my love of history.

First published 2017
This paperback edition published 2020

The History Press
97 St George's Place, Cheltenham,
Gloucestershire, GL50 3QB
www.thehistorypress.co.uk

British Library Cataloguing in Publication Data.
A catalogue record for this book is available from the British Library.

ISBN 978 0 7509 9375 3

Typesetting and origination by The History Press
Printed and bound in Great Britain by TJ International Ltd.

CONTENTS

ABOUT THE AUTHOR

NATASHA SHELDON studied Ancient History and Archaeology at the University of Leicester and liked the city so much that she stayed. She is a full-time author and history columnist. She is the author of *Not a Guide to Leicester* and *Leicester in 100 Dates*, both published by The History Press.

INTRODUCTION

The name *Lægrecastrescir* was first recorded in 1087, but Leicestershire is so much older.

To the Saxons it was the kingdom of Mercia. To the Romans before them it was at the hub of Roman Britain. To the Celts it was the land of the Corieltauvi, also called Coritani, a fierce, warlike tribe. To the Vikings, it was part of the Danelaw.

Leicestershire has so often been the backdrop for many of the turning points in British history. Kings have been killed and buried here, and royal dynasties have changed hands. Leicestershire has been the birthplace of rebels and heroes, movers and shakers, who have changed Britain and even the world.

Leicestershire's land has a unique character, shaped long ago. Its geology has dictated the industries that have made Leicestershire's towns great and the foods that have made the county famous.

Leicestershire has always been a meeting place of people and a melting pot of cultures – from prehistory to the present day. It is one of Britain's most diverse counties, and its most recent incomers have only enriched the county's many traditions.

To include everything about Leicestershire in a book of this size is impossible. Instead, I have tried to concentrate on producing a potted history. I've chosen whimsical, amusing, little known and occasionally disturbing tales, facts and anecdotes that illustrate just what makes Leicestershire unique.

I hope that this brief journey through Leicestershire's past and present will amuse and inform in equal measure.

1

NATURAL LEICESTER

THE MAKING OF LEICESTERSHIRE

Leicestershire marks the centre of England – or rather, the geographical centre of England is in Leicestershire. This landmark spot is at Ordnance Survey ref. SP 36373.66 96143.05, which falls at Lindley Hall Farm, near Fenny Drayton and Higham.

The county shares its borders with Rutland, Nottinghamshire, Northamptonshire, Warwickshire, Derbyshire, Lincolnshire and Staffordshire. According to the Office for National Statistics, in 2018 there were 208,378 hectares of farmland, woodland and towns within those borders.

But this wasn't always the case.

THE STORY OF THE LAND

In the beginning, there was lava – lots of lava.

Some 600 million years ago, Precambrian Leicestershire was submerged under a shallow sea, studded with volcanic islands. The islands constantly spewed out ash and lava, which eventually formed the county's oldest layers of igneous rock. These rocks, visible in the Charnwood region around Blackbrook Reservoir and Swithland Wood, are one of England's few exposures of Precambrian rock.

Bardon Hill, an extinct volcano in north-west Leicestershire, is a relic of those times. It is also the highest point in Leicestershire, reaching 912ft above sea level. John Curtis, a nineteenth-century entomologist, described it as 'one of the most extraordinary points of view in nature.' Even today, the view from the hill's summit in clear weather allows views of Shropshire, the Malvern Hills and not-so-distant Lincoln Cathedral, according to the *Leicester Mercury*.

Time passed. The primal sea retreated, and the mud it left behind began to form into Leicestershire's famous Swithland Slate. Not long afterwards, the magmas began to cool to create the pink and grey granite of Mountsorrel, which in the 1970s and '80s was the location of the largest quarry in Europe.

About 420 million years ago Leicestershire and the rest of the landmass it occupied was on the move. This seismic relocation wrinkled the land. In Leicestershire, one of these folds survives as the Thringstone Fault, which forms the eastern border between the Leicestershire and Derbyshire coalfield.

These coalfields formed during the Carboniferous period, when the warm primal seas that had re-flooded the land drained to become swamps and forests, which in their turn died away to become peat, which eventually transformed into coal. At the same time, limestone deposits were forming around the area of Grace Dieu.

At the end of this era the rivers took over, depositing fluvial deposits to form Shepshed Sandstone.

Further west, much of Leicestershire's landscape is mainly made up of deposits of boulder and Lias clay, dropped by busy glaciers during the last ice age. The ice formed many of Leicestershire's valleys such as the Vale of Belvoir. Just north of the Vale is the lowest point in Leicestershire, where the land dips to 24.8m above sea level. It can be found just along a bend in a minor road near Bottesford and the River Devon, near the county border with Nottinghamshire.

FOSSILS AND DINOSAURS

THE LEICESTER MAMMOTH

On 28 October 1863, a strange object was found during the construction of a sewer off Belgrave Road.

The object was 9ft 7in long and 2ft in circumference. It would have been longer but unfortunately, the workmen who discovered it unwittingly 'lost' 2–3ft of it before they realised that they had something unusual on their hands.

The workmen were unsure quite what it was they had found – only that it was not contemporary. After some debate, they settled on it being an old Roman column, but called in the experts to be on the safe side.

The 'column' was sent to a local geologist, Mr James Plant, who declared it to be part of the tusk of *Elephas primigenius* – a mammoth.

An excited Mr Plant hotfooted it to the site and was fortunate to find the ground undisturbed. The workmen had discovered the tusk on a 3ft layer of red marl dating to around 180 million years previously. However, Plant concluded that the beast was not contemporary with this layer. Instead, its body had sunk through younger, softer gravel above, until it came to rest on the more ancient layers. This discovery dated the mammoth to 20,000 years ago.

The Leicester mammoth made national headlines, with even *The Times* taking an interest in the doings of the Leicester drain. Experts arrived and declared that based on the curvature of the fragment and its 'nearly uniform thickness', the tusk would originally have been 16ft long – even larger than the specimen in the British Museum.

THE BARROW KIPPER

Barrow upon Soar is famous for a plesiosaur of the species *Rhomaleosaurus megacephalus* – nicknamed the 'Barrow Kipper' – excavated there in 1851. The dinosaur was found in a lime pit outside the village.

The skeleton is on display at the New Walk Museum and Art Gallery in Leicester, with a full-size replica on display at Charnwood Museum in Loughborough. But Barrow marks the Kipper in its own way, with a sign on the roundabout in the centre of the village commemorating its oldest resident.

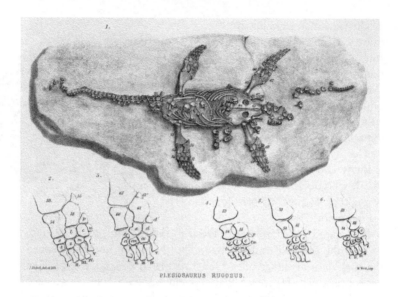

PLESIOSAURUS RUGOSUS.

CHARNIA MASONI

Charnwood Forest was the site of the first ever-recorded discovery of *Charnia masoni*, the earliest known large, complex fossilised species on record.

The fossil was named after the place it was found and its finder, local schoolboy Roger Mason. In 1957, Roger and some friends were exploring a quarry near the Charnwood village of Woodhouse Eaves when he discovered imprints in a rock like the fronds of a fern.

The imprint turned out to be neither plant nor animal but a kind of pre-animal, the first evidence that complex multicellular life existed in the Precambrian period. Charnwood is the only place in Western Europe where these Precambrian fossils have been found.

RIVERS AND WATERWAYS

The River Soar is Leicestershire's principal river, bisecting the county from north to south. The Soar's name comes from *ser* – to flow – which it shares with other European rivers such as the Seine.

The source of the Soar in Leicestershire is between Hinckley and Lutterworth. From there, the river runs down through the county to Leicester, along the fertile Soar Valley until it joins the River Trent at the county boundary at Trent Lock.

During the Industrial Revolution, the Soar turned a most unnatural shade of pink due to discharges from Leicester's textile industry. However, a clean-up by the Environment Agency has returned the river to its natural shade and today industrial discharges are carefully monitored.

In 2004, the *Telegraph* reported how 250,000 requests to the Environment Agency from Leicestershire Sikhs and Hindus led to permission being granted for the Soar to stand in for the Ganges River at funerals. The reason for this request was to avoid the prohibitive costs of travelling to India to use the original sacred river.

The Soar has several tributaries, namely Soar Brook, Thurlaston Brook, the River Biam, Rothley Brook, Black Brook, Whetstone Brook, the River Sence, the River Wreake and Kingston Brook.

THE RIVERS WREAKE AND EYE

This major tributary of the River Soar is, in fact, two rivers in one. For the 6 miles before it reaches Melton Mowbray, the river is known as the Eye, but once past the town, it changes in name and character to become the Wreake.

The clue to this dual naming is in the meaning of the words. The initial stretch of the waterway is calm and unremarkable, hence 'Eye', which comes from the Old English *ēa* or 'the river'.

The Norse invaders of the eighth century were clearly more impressed with the latter stretch, which gave them great trouble and led them to rename it as the Wreake, after their word for twisting and meandering.

ROTHLEY BROOK

Rothley Brook forms a southern boundary around Charnwood Forest, beginning at Bagworth and ending when it joins the River Soar at Rothley, the place after which it is named today, although once it was known as 'Heather Brook' or 'Great Brook'.

The brook is a haven for birds and wildlife, with over forty species of birds identified including kingfishers, great spotted woodpeckers and little and tawny owls.

THE RIVER SENCE

The Sence has its origins at Copt Oak in Leicestershire before leaving the county and joining the River Anker on the Warwickshire border. In the nineteenth century, there were at least eight watermills along the river.

THE RIVER SMITE

The Smite originates from several springs near Holwell, one of Leicestershire's many chalybeate springs. In the seventeenth and eighteenth centuries the water from the spring was considered to have healing properties and was laid out with stone seating for those that took the waters. The spring contains iron salts, which give it a reddish colour, and it is considered to have a distinctive sulphur taste.

THE RIVER MEASE

The River Mease and the lower part of one of its tributaries, the Gilwiskaw (pronounced *jill-a-whiskey*) Brook, are both protected as 'one of the best examples of an unspoilt meandering lowland river'.

GROBY POOL

Lying on the edge of Charnwood Forest, Groby Pool is the largest expanse of open water in the county. It may not all be natural, however, as it seems to owe its formation to Roman clay extraction and the damming of the slate brook by medieval monks from Leicester Abbey.

FLOODS

Flooding is not a modern phenomenon in Leicestershire. In May 1932, the village of Croft became waterlogged following three to four days of continuous rain. The ground could finally hold no more water and inhabitants were stranded in the upper storeys of their homes as the water levels rose, with rescuers having to reach them by boat.

In Wymeswold, the River Mantle would also regularly break its banks. The flooding was so bad that boys would launch a boat down the aptly named Brook Street, which was, in fact, the village's main road.

In 1881, an Improvement Act meant Leicester's corporation could build flood defences to protect the town and its outlying areas from the floods that periodically plagued it.

Unfortunately, the defences were not completed in time to deal with the heavy rainfall of March 1889. The rain had been falling for days, but on 8 March it intensified. The land was waterlogged, and the timber sleepers used in the half-finished flood defences were washed downstream by the swollen waters. They eventually came to a halt, causing a blockage that resulted in the very flood they were meant to prevent.

By 3 p.m. that afternoon, low-lying areas such as Oxford Street and Aylestone Road were under water, with factory cellars so severely flooded that the premises had to close. By 6 p.m. town residents were taking refuge in upstairs rooms as 'the streets themselves assumed the character of canals'.

OTHER LEICESTERSHIRE RIVERS

River Avon	River Chater	Derwent Mouth	River Jordan
River Swift	River Tweed	River Whipling	

FORESTS AND WOODS

According to the Woodland Trust, only 5.82 per cent of Leicestershire is wooded, with just 0.84 per cent of that composed of ancient woodland. Leicestershire has over 100 woods in this category – and that's not including the national forests and other woodlands still in progress.

CHARNWOOD FOREST

Seven miles north-west of Leicester, Charnwood Forest occupies the oldest bedrocks in the county. Its name derives from *cerne woda*, from the Celtic *carn*, meaning cairn, and the Old English *wudu*, meaning wood.

The forest is an important recreational area, with woodland walks noted for their displays of bluebells in the early spring, rock climbing and hillwalking. Popular places with public access include Bardon Hill, Beacon Hill, Bradgate Park, Swithland Wood and the Outwoods, and Stoneywell Cottage.

THE NATIONAL FOREST

In 1990, Charnwood Forest acquired a new neighbour. The new National Forest is part of a Countryside Commission incentive to increase woodland in low-forested areas.

The forest, which also spans Derbyshire and Staffordshire, covers Leicestershire in the old industrial areas of Coalville, Swadlincote and Ashby de la Zouch. By 2013, the National Forest had spread sufficiently to increase forestation in the affected regions to 16.5 per cent – and it continues to grow.

JUBILEE WOODS

As the name suggests, these 10 hectares of mixed woodland surrounding Beacon Hill Country Park were presented to the city council in 1977 to commemorate Her Majesty the Queen's Silver Jubilee.

The woodland was expanded in 2012 to coincide with the Diamond Jubilee. The Woodland Trust also announced that sixty new woods were to be planted across the UK, one for every year of Queen Elizabeth II's reign.

OTHER LEICESTERSHIRE WOODS

Eye Brook Valley Woods
Martinshaw Wood
Sarah's Wood
Coleorton Wood
Great Merrible Wood
Cloud Wood
Burbage and Sheepy Woods
Owston Woods
Leighfield Forest

Hangingstone and Outwoods
Bagworth Heath Woods
Sheet Hedges Wood
Sence Valley Forest Park
Tugby Wood
Allexton Wood
Grace Dieu Woods
Asplin Woods

PARKS, NATURE RESERVES AND SITES
OF SPECIAL SCIENTIFIC INTEREST

In January 2018, Leicestershire had seventy-six Sites of Special Scientific Interest (SSSI) and several nature reserves. Here are just a selection.

AYLESTONE MEADOWS

The city of Leicester's largest nature reserve and area of open space lies on the floodplains of the Rivers Soar and Biam. During the summer months, it is the grazing area for a herd of rare Leicestershire Longhorn cattle. In 2011–12, more than 600 species of plants and animals were found on the site, including a previously unknown species of willow tree. According to Leicestershire and Rutland Wildlife Trust, the tree, which is a cross between goat willow, grey willow, purple willow and osier willow, is unique.

According to nature experts, these finds make Aylestone Meadows a 'most extensive area of wildlife'. But these rare species and the meadows themselves could have been lost. In 2011, Leicester City Council planned to build a floodlit football pitch over them – until the resulting outpouring of local feeling changed their minds.

TILTON RAILWAY CUTTING AND OTHER INTERESTING SITES

This disused railway cutting is a window into Leicestershire's geological past. Tilton's rock cliffs, although overgrown, reveal some of the oldest exposed rocks in Leicestershire, with ironstone and limestone sediments dating back almost 200 million years. The site is also a rich source of fossils, especially brachiopods, which has led to it being declared a geological Site of Special Scientific Interest.

But the rocks of Charnwood Lodge are older still. Covering 80 hectares of land, the site has rock formations dating back 600 million years – amongst the oldest in England.

The rocks date from Leicestershire's volcanic era, when they jostled each other in the pyroclastic flow of the county's Precambrian volcanoes. Age aside, it is rare to find rocks formed in this way, making it a geologist's heaven and a site of scientific interest.

Charnwood Lodge is also home to rare plant life and it is one of the few sites in Leicestershire and Rutland to host the lemon-scented and the hard species of fern. It is also the only place in the county to have an example of the alpine fungus *Melanoleuca evenosa*.

Nearby Beacon Hill Country Park, near Loughborough, covers over 100 hectares of grassland and woodland. It is a popular spot for walking and climbing, being the second-highest point in Leicestershire at 248m.

The park contains a collection of native trees, first planted in 1996. Many of the trees are labelled, and several boxes provide audio commentaries of biological and historical interest on selected tree species.

For rare plant life, the 9 hectares of Muston Meadows cannot be beaten. Muston is the finest lowland meadow in England and plays host to thirty-three types of grass and over 100 other species of flowering plant, most notably 10,000 green-winged orchids.

Dimminsdale, a former lead and limestone mine, has been reclaimed by natural heathland to form a paradise for rare species and areas of broadleaf woodland. The old mine pits form pools fed by nearby streams and the meadows are home to sheep fescue, heath grass, heath bedstraw and harebell.

OTHER CONSERVATION SITES, PARKS AND NATURE RESERVES

Lount Nature Reserve

Brocks Hill Country Park

Watermead Country Park

Charnwood Lodge National Nature Reserve

Fosse Meadows Nature Area

Market Bosworth Country Park

Broombriggs Farm and Windmill Hill

Donisthorpe Woodland Park

Castle Hill Country Park

Leighfield Forest

Swithland Wood

River Mease

Burbage Common

River Eye

Bradgate Park

Ashby Woulds Trail

Melton Country Park

NATURAL PHENOMENON …

Even today Leicestershire can be affected by the wonders of nature – from above and below.

EARTHQUAKES

1750 was a year of earthquakes about the British Isles. At around noon on 30 September 1750, Leicestershire was affected by the strongest earthquake of the year.

Although relatively mild in earthquake terms, the quivering earth caused some alarm. In Leicester, people heard a rushing noise and for a minute or two houses undulated, with chimney pots and slates thrown from the roofs. The only serious injury occurred to a child just outside the town, who was thrown from a chair into a fire and 'somewhat burnt'.

METEOR STORMS

On 14 November 1866, Leicestershire was treated to a grand meteoric shower between midnight and 2 a.m. – or rather it would have been if it hadn't been so cloudy.

The countrywide phenomena were reported by *The Illustrated London News* and *Symonds Monthly Meteorological Magazine*. While in the south of the country people gazed in wonder as the celestial rocks cascaded down to earth through clear skies, in Leicestershire it was a rather more dark and stormy occasion, although the veil of cloud and tempestuous conditions also added to the drama of the event. Gaps in the cloud allowed tantalising glimpses of the bright and 'very numerous' meteors, framed by flashes of lightning and driving rain as they descended to earth.

On Christmas Eve 1965, Barwell and Earl Shilton were treated to a very special Christmas light show when meteor fragments – one the size of a Christmas turkey – showered the region!

One meteorite hit a car, destroying the engine. When the owner of the vehicle attempted to claim on his insurance, the company replied that it was an 'act of God' and would not pay. So, the man wrote another letter, this time addressed to 'Dear Mr God'. However, he had no more luck with the heavenly authorities than he did with the earthly ones.

RARE RAINBOWS

The Smile in the Sky

In July 2011, the sky appeared to be literally smiling down on the residents of Market Bosworth when an upside-down rainbow appeared above the town.

This 'smile in the sky' – or a circumzenithal arc to give it its correct name – was not unknown but most unexpected, in Leicestershire at least. 'Circumzenithal arcs are seen relatively rarely in Britain because they can only be seen at the right combination of atmospheric conditions,' said a Met Office spokesperson.

So, what are the right atmospheric conditions? Much colder than would be expected in July, certainly, as the circumzenithal arc is usually only found in polar regions!

Leicester's Rainbow Cloud

In February 2016, the people of Leicester were amazed to see an unusual phenomenon in the sky. An oval of bright rainbow-shaped light was observed above the city, described as a 'rainbow cloud'.

Leicester Mercury weatherman Dave Mutton explained that the cloud was the product of the meeting of a warm and cold front. This occurrence caused bits of the cloud to break up, with the rainbow occurring in the break in the cloud cover. 'It is a very dramatic illustration of what happens when two different temperatures of air meet,' said Dave. 'Earlier in the day we had warmer air from the north-west, which produced a few showers. This air then met colder air which swept in.'

... AND UNNATURAL PHENOMENON

THE VARDY QUAKE

In February 2016, Leicester City fans literally made the earth move at the King Power stadium when their joy caused an earthquake.

The fans were celebrating the Foxes last-minute winning goal in a match against Norwich. At the time, a seismometer was in residence at the football ground, one of several planted by the University of Leicester as part of a scheme to measure earthquakes around the world.

In the final minutes of the match, instead of recording an earthquake caused by movements of the earth's crust, the seismometer measured the fans making the earth move as their eruption of joy caused a quake that measured at a magnitude of 0.3 – a minor earthquake!

'It wasn't just a case of cheering or clapping, it was 30,000 people standing up at the same time – an awful amount of energy,' said one of the researchers in explanation.

The 'earthquake' has been nicknamed the 'Vardy Quake' in honour of Leicester City's top scorer, Jamie Vardy.

2

TOWN AND COUNTRY

THE LIE OF THE LAND

The city of Leicester aside, Leicestershire is divided into seven distinct regions. These consist of four boroughs: Hinckley and Bosworth, Charnwood, Oadby and Wigston, and Melton, and three districts: Blaby, Harborough and North West Leicestershire.

BOUNDARIES AND BORDERS

The boundaries of Leicestershire haven't changed much with time, probably because many are naturally determined. Since Saxon times, the River Trent has marked the northern border with Derbyshire. Here, the traditional crossing place between the two counties was established at King's Mill in 1009 by a charter of Ethelred the Unready.

Elsewhere, roads determine the county limits. Prehistoric Sewstern Lane is the long-established boundary between Leicestershire and Lincolnshire, dividing not only the two counties but also the village of Sewstern itself.

To the west, the Roman road of Watling Street divides Leicestershire from Warwickshire. Rutland was a part of Leicestershire briefly between 1974 and 1997: now Ermine Street acts as a divider between the two counties.

ALL CHANGE

Towns have also moved in and out of Leicestershire. Snibston and the area around Measham and Donisthorpe used to be part of Derbyshire until they moved in 1884 and 1897 as part of the Counties Act. The latter two towns were part of a swap: Leicestershire parted with Netherseal and Overseal as its part of the exchange.

Elsewhere, Leicestershire simply swallowed up parts of other counties. A burgeoning Market Harborough expanded so much that it encroached upon the Northamptonshire village of Little Bowden. The village's journey from one county to the other occurred slowly. In 1891, only part of the village was deemed to be in Leicestershire, but by 1927 the transition was complete.

THE SYMBOLS OF LEICESTERSHIRE

Leicestershire County Council were granted their coat of arms on 25 January 1930. The arms are quartered to display the emblems of four important county families: the ermine cinquefoil of the Beaumont family, established by the first Norman earl, Robert de Beaumont; the double-tailed white lion of Simon de Montfort; the ermine plume of John of Gaunt, through whose son, Henry IV, Leicestershire passed into the royal estates; and finally the black sleeve of the Hastings family, landowners and prolific builders of castles.

The importance of the countryside to Leicestershire is also reflected. Supporting the arms are a sheep and a black bull, representing the county's original industries of wool and grazing. Cresting the arms is a fox, representing the importance of fox hunting to the county.

People often assume this coat of arms is the county flag of Leicestershire. This is not the case. In fact, Leicestershire is currently the only remaining English county without a registered county flag.

The campaign for Leicestershire to have a flag encompassing the county and the city of Leicester began in earnest in 2016 when Professor Graham Shipley of the University of Leicester and a group of enthusiastic locals launched their campaign for 'A Flag for Leicestershire'. In 2019, the group submitted their proposed design to The Flag Institute in London, which incorporates the familiar cinquefoil from the county council and city flags with the Leicestershire fox. The race is now on to ensure Leicestershire finally has its own banner.

LEICESTERSHIRE'S POPULATION

THE FIRST PEOPLE

Evidence suggests that the land that would become Leicestershire was occupied as early as the Palaeolithic period. Early habitation was small-scale and scattered. It seems that very early man was living and making stone tools on the banks of the River Bytham at Brooksby Quarry near Melton Mowbray as early as 950,000–450,000 years ago. Late Palaeolithic flint-knapping at Bradgate Park suggests that this area was also inhabited, however sporadically, possibly as a hunting camp.

THE WELBY HOARD

By the Bronze Age, it seems Leicestershire was attracting immigrants. In the late nineteenth century, the Welby Hoard was discovered near to some of the major prehistoric routes that bisected Britain. The hoard consisted of axes, swords, a bowl and a bronze cauldron, all in a central European style unmatched anywhere else in Britain.

Although thought to be a scrap metal collection, the well-used weapons with their European design suggest the hoard was deposited by people living locally who had come from abroad, rather than items acquired through passing trade.

THE POPULATION TODAY

Today, we can say with greater certainty from where the people of Leicestershire originate. The 2011 census shows the county had a total population of 650,489 people. Of this. 578,432 were white British and 12,807 from other white groups.

In the city of Leicester, just over half of the population describe themselves as white British, compared to 80 per cent nationally – meaning Leicester just missed out on being the first British city with a minority white population.

The largest of Leicestershire's ethnic groups are Asian British, followed by other Asian groups, black British, Chinese, mixed white and Asian, and mixed white and black.

Seventy per cent of Leicestershire's ethnic population live in an urban context, with 18 per cent on the fringes of cities or in towns and 12 per cent in villages. Urbanites concentrate in the major settlements of Loughborough, Ashby de la Zouch, Market Harborough, Melton Mowbray, Oadby, Wigston and Lutterworth. Leicester is the main settlement of choice, mainly because of the employment opportunities it offers.

Large-scale immigration began after Indian Independence in the late 1940s. Ten million people became dislocated as tensions caused by the subsequent split of the subcontinent caused intercommunity violence. The British Nationality Act 1948 technically gave every Commonwealth citizen the right to move to Britain, making it a natural choice for those seeking a refuge.

Britain also needed the workers. So, many Indians and Pakistanis began to buy homes in Leicester's Spinney Hill and Belgrave areas where houses were most affordable.

But the 1970s saw the greatest influx when Idi Amin, President of Uganda, expelled all Asians from the country. Most of these immigrants settled in Leicester. Between 1968 and 1978, the city received 20,000 displaced Asian Africans, who once again settled in the most affordable areas, namely around Highfields, Belgrave Road and Rushey Mead.

TOWNS AND VILLAGES

THE FIRST TOWNS

The first concrete evidence for substantial settlement in Leicestershire comes from the Neolithic period. Husbands Bosworth has the oldest Scheduled Monument in the county, dating back to 3000 BC. The single-causewayed enclosure, complete with late Neolithic pottery and arrowheads discovered in its ditch, was probably a ritual site rather than a settlement. But in order to build and maintain it, organised groups of people had to be living nearby.

Evidence for Neolithic settlement does, however, exist at the other end of the county. Appleby Magna possesses the remains of a substantial 6-acre enclosure situated next to the River Mease, consisting of an oval ditch surrounding several roundhouses. Misterton with Walcote also displays ploughed out enclosures or barrows dating to the early Neolithic era. But Croft has the earliest potential habitation site for this period, with the possible remains of postholes from houses dating to the late Mesolithic/ early Neolithic period.

Evidence of an established, hierarchical society is suggested by the 250–300 suspected Bronze Age barrows in Leicestershire. The barrow cemetery near Lockington in north-west Leicestershire is one of the most impressive – if only for its gold hoard.

The hoard was found in the ditch of one of the barrows, although the mounds themselves are gone, identified only by crop marks. Its pottery vessels and copper dagger accompany two bracelets made of thin sheet gold – some of the earliest examples of gold work in the British Isles.

Charcoal and charred bone found during excavations in the early 1990s suggest funerary activity in an earlier period, with the barrow built later over the remains. Clearly, Lockington was a sacred site of some long-standing and would need to have been maintained by local settlements.

Examples of Bronze and Iron Age settlements can be found at Heather and Melton Mowbray. By now, Leicestershire was part of the tribal lands of the Corieltauvi, who occupied most of the East Midlands by the time of the Roman conquest.

But it is Leicestershire's hill forts that can be said to be its first towns. Centres of commerce and defence, they are, according to archaeologist Dr Jeremy Taylor, lecturer of Landscape Archaeology at the University of Leicester, 'the nearest thing to a town before places like Leicester ever existed'.

Situated along the ancient Salt Way, which runs from Winchester to the Humber, Beacon Hill's fort has natural defences that were supplemented with man-made ditches and banks.

Its proximity to the road and the finds within the hill fort itself suggest it was more than just a defensive site. A socketed axe, axe mould, a bronze bracelet and two spearheads found in a pit indicate a centre of production or trade that would have required long-term, permanent occupation.

Stone axes dating to 3000 BC demonstrate that the strategic location of Breedon Hill in north-west Leicestershire made the site the perfect settlement for Neolithic man. Sadly, quarrying has largely destroyed the site, but pits, quern stones and postholes remain, suggesting the location was occupied permanently for a lengthy period – probably into the Iron Age.

South of Melton Mowbray is Burrough Hill, Leicestershire's largest hill fort, which again enjoyed its heyday in the Iron Age. The fort was well secured, with a defensive rampart that extended inwards as a tunnel leading to a double gateway and a guard chamber. Inside, there are signs of trade activities. But most significant of all, geophysical surveys by the School of Archaeology at the University of Leicester have identified roundhouses within the enclosure. Most unusual of all, it seems the hill remained occupied for the first century of the Roman occupation.

THE HALLATON HOARD

It seems Leicestershire was in contact with Rome long before it sent its soldiers to conquer. The Hallaton Hoard is the largest hoard of British Iron Age coins – but it seems to have quite a few Roman ones too!

The hoard consisted of over 5,000 silver and gold coins, 4,835 minted by the Corieltauvi. But in amongst this native small change was a Roman parade helmet, jewellery, and quite a few Roman coins. One, a silver denarius, dates to 211 BC, making it the oldest coin in Roman Britain.

Professor David Mattingly of the University of Leicester believes the hoard indicates contact between Leicestershire and Rome before the lands of the Corieltauvi was conquered.

RATAE CORIELTAUVORUM

When the Roman legions finally arrived in Britain, they established what we recognise today as towns. One of those settlements still survives under the modern name of Leicester. But to the Romans it was *Ratae Corieltauvorum* – 'the ramparts of the Corieltauvi'.

By the second century AD, *Ratae* was a model Roman town with bathhouses, grid pattern streets, temples, civic buildings and fine villas that spoke of a substantial *municipium* at the centre of the Romano-British trade route. The remains of its baths at Jewry Wall form the largest piece of standing Roman masonry in Britain.

But not every Roman town survived the test of time.

LOST PLACES

Fragments of lost Roman Leicestershire appear to tantalise from time to time. Upper Leighs at Drayton boasts the remains of a fine Roman villa complete with bathhouse and mosaic floors, as well as a rare silver and gold carnelian intaglio ring from the third century. At Ab Kettleby, the remains of a Roman villa's mosaic floor was discovered under the parish church, while remains of a Roman farm and temple at Appleby hint at a further unknown, unnamed town, now lost.

We can only guess at the lost settlements these buildings represent. But not all of Rome's lost places have mislaid their names.

VENONAE

Between AD 43 and AD 409, Venonae was a thriving Roman town. The only written record of its name remains preserved in the *Antonine Itinerary*, a third-century travelogue for holidaying Roman emperors, which hints at Venonae's position by its distance from other Roman towns:

Iter II, the route from Hadrian's Wall to Richborough in Kent, as Venonis, 12 miles from Manduessedum (Mancetter, Warwickshire) and 17 miles from Bannaventa (Whilton Lodge, Northhamptonshire).

Iter VI, the route from London to Lincoln, again as Venonis, 8 miles from Tripontium (Cave's Inn, Warwickshire) and 12 miles from Ratae (Leicester, Leicestershire).

Iter VIII, the route from York to London, once more as Venonis, again 12 miles from Leicester, though this time 18 miles from Whilton Lodge.

From this, we can deduce that Venonae was a station town; a resting point for travellers along the nearby Watling Street and Fosse Way. With the Roman evacuation of Britain, the traffic died and so did the town.

Today, Venonae's location is marked by the settlement of High Cross, near Wigston Parva. As for the town itself, all that remains are Roman coins, the stone foundations of its buildings, scattered tesserae from mosaic floors, roof tiles, and the flues from long-gone central heating systems.

TRIPONTIUM

Situated near Shawell, near Market Harborough, Tripontium lay to the west of Watling Street, the modern A5. Tripontium's position along a major road meant it was well connected to the main Roman road network of Britain.

The town was established as a military post soon after the Roman invasion of Britain in AD 47. Its name refers to the three bridges built over the River Avon and two of its tributaries at the town.

Tripontium prospered for 400 years before being abandoned in the fourth century AD. Rugby Archaeological Society has been excavating the site since 1961 after they realised what they initially thought to be a small wayside settlement was something rather more. The remains of a sizable civilian town began to reveal itself, with large public bathhouses, an administrative building, and a *mansio* or inn.

Temples and a forum are believed to still lie hidden, but Tripontium has revealed some unique finds such as a late Roman bronze belt buckle, adorned with early Christian symbols, and tiles covered in Latin graffiti referring to the Corieltauvi – the native Celtic tribe of the area – and a complete Roman alphabet!

But it is not just Roman settlements that lie lost in Leicestershire.

ANEBEIN

At the time of Domesday, Ambion Hill, which overlooks the battle site at Bosworth, was the site of a thriving country village called Anebein or Hanebein. But by the early fourteenth century, the village was deserted, an early example of depopulation due to the ravages of the Black Death. With the people gone, the village fell into ruin. Local legend says that when the forces of Richard III camped out the night before the Battle of Bosworth, they came across Anebein and found nothing but the ruined church. Those with a keener eye can still make out the ditch that surrounded the 160 by 180m extent of the village, as well as the remains of house platforms.

ELMESTHORPE

Another victim of the plague was the village of Elmesthorpe or Aylmersthorpe, which was inhabited from Roman times. By 1297, Elmesthorpe was home to around forty to fifty farming families when, once again, the Black Death led to severe depopulation and economic failure. People began to leave, and the once-prosperous farming village disappeared.

However, in 1710, people began to return – but not to the old village. Instead, they took the name but established their new settlement away from the site of old Aylmersthorpe, the remains of which are visible from the new village church.

INGARSBY

Ingarsby, 6 miles from Leicester, just north of Houghton on the Hill, is one of the best-preserved deserted medieval villages in England and the site is designated a scheduled monument.

In 1086, thirty-two families were reported living in the village, but as time went on numbers dropped and by 1381 the village was home to only a dozen families.

The village was finally lost in 1469 when Leicester Abbey enclosed the land and turned it over to sheep and cattle. All that remains of the once-thriving settlement today are rectangular mounds that once were houses and hollow trackways that define the village's lost streets and lanes.

BRADGATE

There was once a village in what is now Bradgate Park. The site of two houses are known, but it appears that the village was a scattered settlement rather than tightly packed around a central church. Perhaps this was why it was destroyed, as it would have been difficult to establish a deer park around such a dispersed settlement. But it may equally be because the owner of the land, Thomas Grey, did not want to be such near neighbours with his tenants when he began to build Bradgate House.

Either way, the villagers were evicted and their homes destroyed. In 1500, Thomas Grey received a summons for depopulation. However, he was absolved as he claimed he had housed the displaced villagers elsewhere – which indeed he had. The new settlement was not too far away, at a ford near the River Lin. It logically became known as the 'new town', which gradually evolved into its modern name – Newtown Linford.

ALTON AND KNAPTOFT

Like Bradgate, Alton ceased to exist when the landowner decided the land could be put to better use. The village, which was situated between Coalville and Ashby, became a monastic grange, with the land turned over to sheep rather than people. It was one of only four villages deserted in Leicestershire for this reason, the others being Dishley, Ringlethorp and Weston.

Likewise, Knaptoft was deserted in the seventeenth century when the land was enclosed for sheep farming. But it is not quite deserted: some farm buildings and the church remain in use.

WHAT'S IN A NAME?

BEL THE GIANT

If local legends are to be believed, then a doomed giant called Bel was responsible for the naming of at least four Leicestershire villages.

Bel was enjoying a drink with friends on a hill, when he drunkenly boasted that he could make it to the town of Leicester in one leap. So, he saddled up his sorrel mare and prepared to make the jump. The legend says the settlement on the hill was named Mountsorrel to commemorate the start of his journey.

Bel cleared a mill and landed near the River Soar – but some distance from Leicester. This landing place was immortalised with the name 'one leap', which evolved into Wanlip.

Undeterred, Bel continued. But again he stopped short of his target – this time with such force that the landing broke the saddle girths. This earned the third settlement the name Birstall or 'burst all'.

Bel's final landing was the hardest by far. The plucky giant was thrown to the ground before his exhausted mare fell upon him, crushing the life out of him. And he still hadn't made it to Leicester.

Bel was buried where he fell, which explains the name of his final destination: Bel's Grave, later known as Belgrave.

THE GRIFFIN IN THE WELL

Another legend claims that the hamlet of Griffydam, near Worthington, derived its name from its chalybeate well's unusual guardian.

The sacred spring in question was just off the village's main road and jealously guarded by a griffin, until a local priest overcame it.

However, it seems that the true meaning of the village's name is more prosaic. It actually comes from 'Griffin's dam' for the pond and bank that can still be seen in the settlement.

There are other place names in Leicestershire that preserve the origins of settlements or the origins of the people who have lived in them.

CELTIC PLACES

At least two Leicestershire settlements have their Celtic roots preserved in their names. Ratby is of Celtic origin, as evidenced by the inclusion of a variant of *ratae* in its name – the Celtic term for ramparts. Leicester is the other town. Although its name has changed, its original Roman name of *Ratae Corieltauvorum* also paid homage to its Celtic origins.

Such place names are rare now, as many of Leicestershire's settlements were renamed by later invaders.

SAXON INFLUENCES

The Saxons didn't always rename towns and villages, but they did like to leave their mark. Often, Saxon-occupied places ended with the suffix '*ton*' – the old Mercian term for a settlement. Examples include Thrussington, Syston and Cossington.

Other villages were renamed or founded with purely Saxon names. Great Bowden is one of Leicestershire's oldest villages and derives its name from a combination of the Saxon female name 'Bucga' and 'dun', meaning a flat-topped hill. Likewise, Anstey in northern Leicestershire takes its name from the Angle term for a narrow forest track.

However, one particular word used in certain place names indicates that its residents were definitely not Saxon. The 'Walton' part of Walton on the Wolds derives from the word *wealas* – the Saxon term for stranger. This term was applied to places still settled by their original Romano-British inhabitants, demonstrating that not all the previous inhabitants of Leicestershire had been enslaved or driven away.

VIKING NAMES

Norse settlements can be recognised by the suffix '*by*' – the term for a farm or a settlement. Enderby, Oadby and Ingarsby are just three of the fifty-six place names in Leicestershire governed by this rule.

Ingarsby and Oadby also preserve another Viking naming tendency: that of naming settlements after their victorious war chiefs. Ingarsby is one of many places named after Ivar or Ingar the Boneless, one of the leading Viking lords. Oadby became Outi's dwelling after it was wrestled from the Saxons. Kirby Muxloe was named after Caeri, the Dane who founded it.

The Danes did not stop at settlements: they even took to renaming the landscape. The River Wreake took its name from the Danish term for 'twisted' while the Dane Hills commemorate Leicestershire's whole period under the Danelaw.

Some place names combined Danish personal names suffixed with the Saxon '*ton*'. Thrussington, Syston, Cossington and Thurmaston are examples. Humberstone may also be one of these, possibly deriving its name from the Danish leader Ubba or Hubba, the first Viking to seize Leicester. But as with so many names, this is open to debate.

Other Saxon/Danish towns and villages in Leicestershire include:

- **Kegworth:** From the Old English for 'key' or from the enclosure of a Dane called Kaggi or 'Red Beard'.
- **Normanton le Heath:** From the Old English for 'the settlement of northmen on the heath', indicating a village taken over or established by Norse or Danish settlers.
- **Measham:** Originally known as *Meas-Ham*, meaning a settlement on the River Mease.
- **Ravenstone:** The old Norse name *Hrœfnes* and the suffix '*tun*' suggests Ravenstone was an Anglo-Saxon village named after a Norseman called Hrœfnes.
- **Melton Mowbray:** The name Melton comes from the early English word *Medeltone* meaning '*Middletown surrounded by small hamlets*'. But Mowbray dates to Norman times and relates to the early Norman lords of the town.

THE NORMAN CONQUEST

The Normans were content to leave place names as they were – unless they founded them or really wanted a reminder of home. Newton Burgoland was originally known as Neutone or new town of the Burgilon family, the settlement's Norman lords. The name Mountsorrel, despite the claims of the legend of Bel, almost certainly dates to this period, although the settlement it is attached to existed for much longer. It is thought to be named after the French village Montsoreau, near to Fontevraud Abbey, where Henry II was buried.

On the other hand, Stretton en le Field seems to combine all of Leicestershire's historical time periods into one. Although not Roman in itself, it is one of the fifteen Strettons in England set along a Roman road – hence the *stret/straet* element. The Saxons also settled there – hence the '*ton*' in the name, while field or '*feld*' relates to the open country. '*En le*' shows the French influence.

GREAT HOUSES

One thing the Normans and their descendants were responsible for was the founding of many of Leicestershire's great houses.

BELVOIR CASTLE

Situated in the Vale of Belvoir, Belvoir Castle and the vale it overlooks are named after the French word for beautiful view.

The castle also overlooks the villages and towns of Redmile, Woolsthorpe, Knipton, Harston, Harlaxton, Croxton Kerrial, Bottesford and Grantham. The local residents of these settlements stubbornly refused to pronounce the name in the same way as their French overlords. Hence in Leicestershire, 'Belvoir' is always pronounced 'beaver'.

ASHBY DE LA ZOUCH CASTLE

In 1462, Edward IV granted the Norman manor house of Ashby to his Lord Chamberlain, Lord William Hastings. Hastings built an impressive four-storey tower castle there. But he did not live to enjoy it long as Richard III beheaded him in 1483.

However, Ashby de la Zouch Castle survived and played host to Henry VII, Mary Queen of Scots and James and Charles I – until the tower was partially destroyed by Parliamentary forces.

KIRBY MUXLOE CASTLE

A manor house existed at Kirby Muxloe from the thirteenth century. In 1480, the house became another of Lord William Hastings' building projects – one he was doomed never to see through to completion.

Hastings planned to turn the manor house into a fortified castle, complete with towers, walls and a moat. The new construction was built strikingly from brick, which was expensive, but was the new 'must have' building material for any late-medieval home improvements.

Perhaps Hastings wanted a fortified home because he was unsettled by the times. Unfortunately for him, his refuge remained incomplete when he met his untimely end.

The remaining Hastings family made the best of the half-finished castle and settled in its completed wing. But in the seventeenth century they abandoned Kirby Muxloe for better things. The castle was used as a farm until it was again abandoned and allowed to fall into picturesque ruins.

BRADGATE HOUSE

Bradgate House was also brick-built and fortified. But unlike Kirby Muxloe Castle, it was completed before trouble struck its owners.

The house was constructed between 1499 and 1520. It was started by Thomas Grey, Marquis of Dorset, and completed by his son. The finished house was 200ft long and had two storeys. A great hall and parlour lay at its core, with the family quarters in the east wing and the service areas in the west.

Bradgate was home to Lady Jane Grey during her childhood and remained in the Grey family until the twentieth century. However, the family abandoned the house during the eighteenth century, when they made their chief residence in Staffordshire.

INDUSTRIAL TOWNS AND VILLAGES

The Industrial Revolution brought about its own changes to Leicestershire, with villages growing in response to the new industries – and new towns arising altogether.

WHITWICK

Whitwick began as a medieval village, listed in the Domesday Book, complete with a castle and annual country fairs. It is unique in that it is the only village in England to contain three cities. The City of Three Waters and the City of Dan are legitimate postal addresses within the village. But the third city's name and location is somewhat elusive. Some locals maintain it is the City of Hockley, while others refer to it simply as 'Hockley'. Its location is vaguer still, with no one knowing for sure exactly where it is, although some speculate it is near to the parish church.

Until the nineteenth century, the village's only industry was framework knitting, but the blossoming of the mining industry transformed Whitwick into a mining town. The old village's buildings, with few exceptions, were swept away to be replaced by Victorian red brick housing.

COALVILLE

At the beginning of the nineteenth century Coalville didn't exist. Instead, the land it would occupy was covered with brambles and gorse, with a country track called Long Lane running down its centre.

Then William Stenson sunk a deep mineshaft on the land and the rest is history. The Whitwick Colliery grew up around the shaft

– and Coalville grew up around the mine. It started in 1824 with a few miners' cottages running down Long Lane. But by 1834 the railway had reached the town and 'Coalville', as it was now known, became linked to Leicester, allowing it to expand its interests into textiles and engineering.

The town did not acquire its name from the mineral responsible for its birth, but from the name of Stenson's large house, 'Coalville', which he built nearby from the proceeds of his mine.

SWANNINGTON AND COLEORTON

SWANNINGTON had been a mining village from the sixteenth century – on a small scale at least, with villagers taking advantage of the exposed coal layers in the area, gathering coal from the nearby fields.

It took the advent of the Leicester and Swannington Railway (L&S) for the village mines to really develop. The ease of transporting coal from the village meant the mines expanded, in turn attracting miners from other areas, leading to massive house building.

But with the growth of nearby Coalville, many miners left equally quickly, leaving Swannington's mining industry to quietly decline. Today, it is a pleasant commuter village.

Like Swannington, COLEORTON was a mining village from the fifteenth century. By the 1420s, it had gained a sufficient reputation for its supply of coal to exchange its original name of Overton Saucy for that of Coal Overton, later shortened to its present form.

The village was the birthplace of mining engineer William Stenson, who expanded mining in the area. So it appears that in more ways than one, Coleorton was key to mining in Leicestershire.

BEST AND WORST

THE SIXTH HAPPIEST PLACE IN THE UK

Blaby was listed as the sixth happiest place in the UK, according to the Office for National Statistics' annual well-being survey for 2014/15. The *Leicester Mercury* reported that the town is the only place in the Midlands to make the top ten in the poll. Good walks, parks and canals, coupled with friendly people and a close community spirit, are cited as Blaby's main attractions by its residents – as well as the 450 clubs and organisations in the area that keep them occupied.

THE MOST DESIRABLE PLACE TO LIVE

According to a Royal Mail survey in 2015, Wigston was the most desirable place to live in Leicestershire. The town won out against its nearest competitors Newtown Linford, Loughborough, Kibworth and Mountsorrel because of its affordable housing, transport links and green spaces.

THE BEST PLACE TO BRING UP CHILDREN

In 2015, Quorn was listed as one of the top five places in the UK to bring up children. According to the *Leicester Mercury*, this is because the village offers 'the peace and space that all children thrive on'. The tranquil countryside around Quorn was also a factor, as was its low crime rate – and the village's excellent schools.

THE WORST PLACE IN ENGLAND TO RAISE A FAMILY

In 2016, Leicester was named the worst place in England to raise a family. The *Leicester Mercury* reported how the uSwitch Better Family Life Index had analysed thirty-three elements of family life across 138 council areas in Britain, including pay, GCSE grades, weather, childcare and access to doctors. The survey claimed the city had fewer primary schools, high council tax, the fourth worst employment level in the UK – and that 43 per cent of Leicester parents were worried they weren't giving their family the best start in life.

But Sir Peter Soulsby, the city's mayor, dismissed the report as having no basis in fact. Instead, he accused uSwitch of 'a cheap bit of marketing' to draw attention to its comparison site services.

Others agreed, with local MPs such as Jon Ashworth defending the city's play areas and children's festivals. 'We have two young children who we are raising in the city,' he said, 'and it is a great place.'

3

MOVERS AND SHAKERS

Many people have helped shape Leicestershire and make it the great county it is today. Likewise, Leicestershire has produced many people who have helped shape the world.

LOCAL LORDS

JOHN OF GAUNT

John of Gaunt was Earl of Leicester as well as Lancaster. He was also the son, brother, uncle and father of kings.

Leicester Castle was reputedly one of his favourite seats. At his death in 1399, his estates passed to his son, Henry Bolingbroke. Bolingbroke's cousin, Richard II, had exiled him, so his newly inherited estates were forfeit. But on his father's death, Henry returned to reclaim his inheritance – and at the same time ousted his cousin from the throne, seizing it for himself.

As Henry IV, Henry's inheritance – which included the whole of Leicestershire – became part of the royal estates.

RICHARD III

On 14 August 1483, Richard III wrote a letter to the King of France 'from my castle in Leicester'. It was the last recorded occupation of the castle by one of its owners.

On his last, fateful visit to Leicester, Richard did not stay in his castle as it was by then too run down. Instead, he stayed in Leicester's plush White Boar Inn – the name reputedly borne by the Blue Boar Inn before Richard's defeat at Bosworth Field – and the rest, as they say, is history. By fighting the last significant battle of the War of the Roses at the Battle of Bosworth and becoming the last English monarch to die in combat, in 1485, Richard III put the county of Leicestershire firmly on the map of British history.

Richard also managed to be ignobly buried and then lost for centuries. But that also worked in Leicestershire's favour, for his rediscovery in 2012 and subsequent reburial in Leicester Cathedral in 2015 has made the county a major tourist hotspot, increasing the local economy in 2015 by 6.6 per cent and leading to the creation of 1,800 new jobs.

SIMON DE MONTFORT

Simon de Montfort was Leicester's sixth earl from 1239 until his untimely death and dismemberment at the Battle of Evesham in 1265.

De Montfort was a major mover and shaker in medieval England. He married Eleanor, the sister of Henry III, and then turned on his brother-in-law, leading the Second Barons' War in 1264, becoming the *de facto* ruler of Britain.

He is also credited with calling two famous parliaments. The first, held in the Great Hall of Leicester Castle, stripped the king of his unlimited authority. Four knights from every county in England were called to attend.

The second parliament, held between January and March 1265, involved ordinary citizens for the first time. As well as knights, two burgesses from each town were summoned. Thus, de Montfort was one of the first advocates of the modern parliamentary system.

In Leicestershire itself, de Montfort improved matters for its people by introducing inheritance by primogeniture instead of ultimogeniture (inheritance by the youngest child). This Leicestershire custom had been impoverishing the county's estates and businesses as, in practice, it meant splitting inheritances among all the deceased's offspring. Primogeniture left the deceased's estate intact and safe in the hands of the eldest child.

One of de Montfort's most shameful acts was to expel the Jews from Leicester in 1231, 'for the good of my soul and the souls of my ancestors and successors'. The expulsion wasn't so much an act of anti-Semitism as a calculated attempt to win the favour of the people of Leicester. Banishing the Jews effectively freed the people of debt, as Jews were the only people who could practise usury.

However, de Montfort's scheme backfired. The Jews didn't go very far. For despite being Earl of Leicester, de Montfort didn't own the whole county. The other half belonged to his great-aunt, Margaret, Countess of Winchester, a fact de Montfort bitterly disputed. The countess probably offered the Jews sanctuary to score a point against her great-nephew.

THE GREYS OF GROBY

The Greys of Groby were notable, if not notorious, for their links to the Crown. That link was first established when John Grey of Groby married Elizabeth Woodville. John died, leaving Elizabeth near destitute with two young sons. A chance encounter with King Edward IV eventually led to their marriage.

Elizabeth's daughter from this marriage, Princess Elizabeth of York, the half-sister of Thomas and Richard Grey, later married Henry Tudor, who became Henry VII. But a few generations later, the Greys links to the Crown were further strengthened by the marriage of Frances, the daughter of Henry VIII favourite sister, Mary, to Henry Grey, the Earl of Suffolk. Their daughter, Lady Jane Grey, the tragic nine-day queen, grew up on the Grey's estate at Bradgate Park.

Henry VIII's will stipulated that if his own children died without issue, the crown was to pass to his sister Mary's descendants – leaving out the Scottish royal family descended from his elder sister Margaret.

After Edward VI's premature death in 1553, unscrupulous nobles sought to raise their profiles by manipulating the will. Edward had been persuaded to make his cousin Jane his heir, over his sisters Mary and Elizabeth. Jane was married to Guildford Dudley, the son of the Duke of Northumberland, and declared Queen.

Mary was joined by her younger sister Elizabeth and, with the help of a popular uprising, regained the support of the Privy Council. Jane and her husband were arrested, after just nine days on the throne.

Mary may have spared Jane's life if it wasn't for the fact that, during her imprisonment in the Tower of London, Sir Thomas Wyatt led a protest against the return of Catholicism – which was joined by Jane's father. As Jane remained a threat as a focus for future Protestant revolts, she was eventually executed in 1554.

After this, the Grey's relationship with the Crown soured. Not only did the family forfeit their barony because of Henry Grey's rebellion, but Elizabeth I also overturned her father's will in favour of the surviving Grey sisters by instead naming James VI of Scotland as her heir.

Perhaps this explains the stance taken by the family during the English Civil War: Thomas Grey, Lord Grey of Groby and MP for Leicester, fought on the side of Parliament and in 1649 was the only aristocratic signatory on the death warrant of Charles I.

REBELS AND POLITICIANS

THOMAS SKEFFINGTON

Thomas Skeffington was High Sheriff of Leicestershire from approximately 1576–77, 1588–89 and 1599–1600. He saw to it that Leicestershire did its bit for Queen and Country by calling upon the county's men to take up arms and defend the nation from the threat of the Spanish Armada.

Some 12,530 men were raised, with 2,000 sent to guard Tilbury Docks while the rest trained in combat in case of invasion.

SIR EVERARD DIGBY

Everard Digby was born around 1576 in Leicestershire to a wealthy landowning family, whose properties included Donington le Heath manor.

Digby, however, was a secret Catholic convert at a time when the faith was under attack. And so, in 1605, despite his popularity at court and being knighted by James I, Digby became part of the Gunpowder Plot, financing and directing from behind the scenes.

If the plan to blow up Parliament was successful, Digby would have been one of the leading players in raising rebellion in the Midlands. Instead, on its failure, he was captured at Holbeche House near Dudley. Despite being the only plotter to plead guilty, he was hung, drawn and quartered on 30 January 1606.

GEORGE VILLIERS

George Villiers was the son of a local Leicestershire landowner who did very well with the Crown and advanced his family into the aristocracy.

Born in 1592 to the second wife of Sir George Villiers of Brooksby Hall near Melton Mowbray, George was the third son and so had no great expectations. But his mother introduced him at court and there in 1614, he quickly caught the eye of the first Stuart king, James I.

James's behaviour with Villiers was an open scandal, with the king openly hugging and kissing the young knight. Whether or not these scandalous feelings were reciprocated is uncertain, but George was quickly promoted, becoming first a baron, then a marquis, next an earl, then Duke of Buckingham and finally, in 1619, Lord High Admiral – despite his lack of prowess in the field.

George remained in favour with James's son, Charles I. Yet he was hated by the Puritans and Parliament because of his military disasters. He was assassinated while at breakfast in 1628, on his way to a further expedition in France. His assassin, an officer called John Felton, declared he killed Villiers because he had 'for so long gone unpunished for his crimes'.

HENRY SMITH AND JOHN COOK

HENRY SMITH was born in Withcote in 1620. He studied law at Oxford and went on to become a Member of Parliament for Leicestershire in 1645.

In 1649, Smith sat as a commissioner for the High Court of Justice at the trial of Charles I. His was the nineteenth signature on the death warrant of the king.

After the Restoration in 1660, Smith was brought to trial for regicide and was sentenced to death. But using his legal prowess, he successfully appealed his sentence, which was commuted to life imprisonment. Smith was committed to the Tower of London until 1664 when he was transported to Jersey, where he died at Mont Orgueil Castle.

JOHN COOK was not so lucky. Born in Burbage in 1608, he too left Leicestershire to study law, eventually becoming Solicitor General of the English Commonwealth.

Cook was in many ways a progressive lawyer. He established a prisoner's right to silence and advocated many reforms to the law, including the abolition of imprisonment for debt, and restrictions on the death penalty for those convicted of theft. Cook recognised that many of those who stole did so out of desperation and he campaigned for probation, rather than hanging, in such cases.

Cook was not an anti-monarchist, but when Charles I began to buck the law, he joined those who tried the king for treason. He led the prosecution, so helping condemn Charles to death. Unlike many, at the Restoration he stood by his actions. Shortly before his death, he wrote to his wife: 'We fought for the public good and would have enfranchised the people and secured the welfare of the whole groaning creation, if the nation had not more delighted in servitude than in freedom.'

He was hung, drawn and quartered on 16 October 1660.

ALICE HAWKINS

Many local Leicestershire women played a significant role in the fight for women's suffrage. One of the most prominent and remarkable was Alice Hawkins.

Alice was born in 1863 and lived most of her life in Leicester. Unlike many others in the suffrage movement, she was working class, a shoe machinist by trade. She was politically active from her teens and became keenly aware that women in her industry had inferior pay and conditions to their male counterparts.

In 1907, she attended her first meeting of the Women's Social and Political Union (WSPU) in Hyde Park, London. That very day, she became active in the movement. Her first spell in prison for her political activities quickly followed. Over the next seven years, she was jailed five times, serving terms in Holloway and Leicester prisons.

After her first sentence was complete, Alice invited Sylvia Pankhurst to speak at Leicester and shortly afterwards the Leicester branch of the WSPU was formed. Alice was the trailblazer – the only person to mount platforms to speak and the only woman to challenge future Prime Minister Winston Churchill when he spoke in Leicester.

She died in Leicester in 1946, aged 83.

THOMAS BABINGTON

Thomas Babington was MP for Leicester from 1800 to 1818, and a leading Anglican evangelical. Educated at St John's College, Cambridge, he worked closely with William Wilberforce on social improvement and the famous bills to abolish the slave trade.

Wilberforce and Babington spent much time at Babington's Rothley retreat working on the text of the bills, and on the analysis of the Select Committee's inquiries into the trade.

BENEVOLENT BENEFACTORS

WILLIAM WYGGESTON

Wyggeston was a successful wool merchant and mayor of Leicester in 1499 and 1510. He also represented Leicester in the seventh parliament of Henry VII.

Wyggeston dedicated a portion of the wealth from his Swannington estate to establish a hospital for the care of the elderly poor. The hospital was set up on land near to Leicester Cathedral. His motives may not have been totally altruistic, as it was common during this period for wealthy men to undertake good works for the

benefit of their soul, but Wyggeston's legacy endured. Although the original building is gone, Wyggeston Hospital continues today – as a retirement home for the elderly on Hinckley Road.

Wyggeston's contribution to the well-being of Leicester's poor is recognised by the inclusion of his figure on Leicester's Haymarket Memorial Clock Tower.

After Wyggeston's death in 1536, his brother, Thomas, continued in his benevolent footsteps by using part of his inheritance to establish a grammar school in Leicester. This school bequeathed its name to the later Wyggeston Grammar School for Boys, which survives now as Wyggeston and Queen Elizabeth I College.

ROBERT SMYTH

Market Harborough's version of Dick Whittington left the town to seek his fortune in 1570. He found work as an archivist with the Lord Mayor of London and eventually became the Chief Comptroller of the City of London.

But Smyth never forgot his roots. He regularly sent money back to his hometown to provide bread for the 'godly, honest poor'. He also established the Old Grammar School in the town, which remained open from 1614 until 1909.

HENRY FEARON

The vicar of All Saints' church, Loughborough, campaigned to bring clean water to the town. When he died in 1885, its grateful people lined the streets of Loughborough in respect.

DR JOHN CHARLES BUCKNILL AND JOHN BUCK

JOHN CHARLES BUCKNILL was born in 1817 at Market Bosworth. After learning of work at the Hanwell Asylum in Middlesex, where patients went without restraints, he became convinced that insanity was a brain disease that could be treated with medication.

Bucknill began to promote and support such treatment as well as promote the civil rights of patients. His work laid the foundations for the more humane treatment of patients in asylums.

In 1853, JOHN BUCK resigned his position as part-time medical officer with Leicestershire Borough Police to become superintendent of the Leicestershire and Rutland County Lunatic Asylum near Victoria Park.

Buck reformed the prison-like environment of the institution, persuading the asylum commissioners to build a washhouse, bakery, chapel, recreation hall, workshops and farm buildings – to service the asylum and provide the inmates with therapeutic employment opportunities. He also instigated regular excursions for the patients and established a brass band.

THOMAS FIELDING JOHNSON

By 1919, the asylum on Victoria Park was no more. Instead, businessman and philanthropist Thomas Fielding Johnson had bought up and donated the site for the establishment of Leicester's own university college, later the University of Leicester. The old asylum building, now the university's administrative block, was named in his honour.

CHARLES BENNION

Although not a native of Leicestershire, Charles Bennion made his fortune from engineering in the county and made it his home. In 1928, he found a way to show the people of Leicestershire just how great his regard for his adopted county was.

That year, the 850-acre Bradgate estate was put up for sale by the Grey family. They had offered it to the people of Leicestershire for public use, but the money to buy the land was not available to the borough. So, Mr Bennion stepped in. He purchased the parkland and, after placing it in trust, formally presented it to the people of Leicestershire as a somewhat late Christmas gift on 29 December 1928.

INTELLECTUALS, SCIENTISTS AND ENGINEERS

HENRY BATES

Born on 8 February 1825, Bates self-educated himself in natural history before leaving Leicestershire for the Amazon, where he remained for eleven years, periodically sending home new specimens. In all, Bates posted back 14,712 species – 8,000 of which were new to science at the time.

But Bates's crucial discovery was that of mimicry in animals. He discovered that hoverflies would imitate the warning noises of wasps and bees to defend themselves against danger. The discovery was named 'Batesian mimicry' in his honour.

THOMAS SIMPSON

Thomas Simpson was born at Market Bosworth in 1710. The son of a weaver, Simpson followed his father into the trade. However, in his free time, he taught himself mathematics.

In his twenties, Simpson graduated from weaving by day and teaching by night to become a full-time mathematician when he moved to London and began lecturing in coffeehouses. By 1743,

Simpson became part of the academic establishment when he was awarded a post at the Royal Military Academy in Woolwich. Two years later, he became a Fellow of the Royal Society.

Simpson is attributed with the invention of 'Simpson's Rule', a formula for estimating the area under a curve. His works include *The Nature and Laws of Chance* and *The Doctrine of Annuities and Reversions*.

SIR FRANK WATSON DYSON

Born in 1868, this Measham Astronomer Royal was noted as an authority on the spectrum of the corona and chromosphere of solar eclipses – and the invention of radio pips. In 1919, during an expedition to observe solar eclipses in South America, he also confirmed Einstein's Theory of Relativity of the effect of gravity on light.

T.E.R. PHILLIPS

Born in Kibworth Harcourt in 1868, this Anglican cleric turned his eyes to the heavens in more than the spiritual sense. During his tenure as a curate and vicar in the south of England, Phillips became an amateur astronomer, with the surface currents of Mars and Jupiter his particular interest.

His expertise was soon recognised, and Phillips became director of the Jupiter section of the British Astronomical Association from 1900 to 1933. Between 1935 and 1940, he branched out to include Saturn in his activities. Phillips became president of the Royal Astronomical Society from 1927 to 1929, having won the Society's Jackson-Gwilt Medal in 1918.

SIR NICHOLAS RIDLEY

Sir Nicholas Harold Lloyd Ridley, inventor of the intraocular lens, was born in Kibworth in 1906. An eye surgeon and consultant, Ridley treated Royal Air Force casualties with eye injuries in the Second World War. He noticed that those with splinters of acrylic plastic from cockpit canopies lodged in their eyes did not have the same inflammatory reaction as those with glass splinters. This led Ridley to develop artificial Transpex lenses to treat cataract patients and on 29 November 1949 he performed the first implant of an intraocular lens. It was not until 1950 that he left a lens permanently in the eye.

Although it took until 1981 for the technique to be widely regarded as safe and effective, cataract extractions using the intraocular lens transplants are now the most common form of eye surgery.

FRANK WHITTLE

Frank Whittle, the inventor of the jet engine, developed some of the world's first jet planes at the British Thomson-Houston works in Lutterworth during the late 1930s and the 1940s. Whittle obtained his first patent for a turbo-jet engine in 1930 and tested it on the ground in 1937. However, Whittle's jet engine did not take to the air until after the outbreak of war. The engine for the UK's first jet aircraft, the Gloster E.28/39, was produced in Lutterworth under Whittle's direction and undertook its maiden flight in May 1941.

EXPLORERS AND ADVENTURERS

CHARLES THROSBY

Charles Throsby was born in Glenfield in 1771, but he made his name much further afield. In 1802, he departed Portsmouth as surgeon aboard a convict transport bound for Sydney, Australia. The voyage was smooth, and it was reported none of the male convicts under Throsby's care died.

Throsby settled in the colony, acting as magistrate and employed as a surgeon and superintendent. But after a brief return visit to England in 1817, he returned to Australia for good and began the exploration of his adopted homeland.

On 8 March 1818, Throsby set out as part of an exploratory group seeking a route to Jervis Bay. Three weeks later, Throsby's section of the party arrived at their destination via the Kangaroo and Lower Shoalhaven rivers. They beat their companions to their destination by asking a pair of passing Aborigines for directions!

Further expeditions followed. In 1819, Throsby pioneered explorations to the west of the Blue Mountains. The rich, fertile land was to be a boon to future settlers and Throsby was awarded a parcel of land at Bong Bong near Moss Vale.

Later, Throsby was put in charge of road construction to the Goulburn Plains, during which time he reached the Yass River and the Murrumbidgee River – again after asking the Aborigines the way.

HISTORIANS, ACADEMICS AND WRITERS

JOHN THROSBY

John Throsby, father of Charles Throsby (see above), was the first historian to write a full history of Leicestershire. He was born on 21 December 1740 in the city of Leicester to alderman Nicholas Throsby and his wife.

John began work as the parish clerk at St Martin's church in Leicester and this gave him the perfect opportunity to begin his studies into the county of his birth. His *Memories of the Town and County of Leicester* – the first full history of the county – contained his own drawings. He was also careful only to include descriptions of sights and events that he had witnessed or had been witnessed by people he interviewed.

Throsby also took a keen interest in local archaeology, as shown by his *Letter to the Earl of Leicester on the Recent Discovery of the Roman Cloaca, or Sewer, at Leicester, with Some Thoughts on Jewry Wall*. He was made a Freeman of Leicester in 1760.

In addition, he was also a great admirer of Richard III, who he viewed as 'one of the greatest heroes England has ever produced' – a view that has only begun to be shared by others in recent times.

Throsby was a trailblazer for the local historians who followed after him. John Nichols described him in his *History and Antiquities of Leicestershire* as 'a man of strong natural genius, who, during the vicissitudes of a life remarkably chequered, rendered himself conspicuous as a draughtsman and topographer'.

ANNA BARBAULD

Anna Laetitia Barbauld (*née* Aikin, 1743–1825) was a poet, essayist and innovative children's author born in Kibworth Harcourt. Thanks to her father John Aikin, she had a classical education denied to many women of the time. Her writings – at a time when it was rare for women to have any sort of successful writing career – also entered the political sphere.

Initially famous for her poems, Barbauld later published *Miscellaneous Pieces in Prose* with her brother, leading many to compare her to Samuel Johnson. After a period teaching in a school with her husband, Barbauld began her most radical political writings during the French Revolution.

When the law granting dissenters full citizenship was defeated in 1790, she wrote *An Address to the Opposers of the Repeal of the Corporation and Test Acts*. She also supported William Wilberforce's anti-slavery stance and, after the defeat of his 1791 attempt to abolish the slave trade, published her *Epistle to William Wilberforce Esq. On the Rejection of the Bill for Abolishing the Slave Trade* as a show of solidarity.

Barbauld's poetry laid the foundation of British romanticism but she fell out of favour in 1812 when she published *Eighteen Hundred and Eleven*, a criticism of Britain's involvement in the Napoleonic Wars. Barbauld was so shocked at its reception that, while she continued to write, she never sought to publish her work again.

BERNARD NEWMAN

Born in 1897 in Ibstock, Newman was a historian, an expert on spies – and the great-nephew of the author George Eliot. He wrote over 100 books of fiction and non-fiction, covering his main areas of interest: travel and politics, mysteries, science fiction and children's books.

Newman's interest in spying stemmed from the First World War, when he was sent undercover to Paris because of his fluency in

French. After the war he became a civil servant but also an avid traveller, visiting over sixty countries before 1939, as well as lecturing across Europe – even meeting Hitler. He witnessed the invasion of France by the Germans and on his return to England joined the Ministry of Information and began writing patriotic novels. He was also sent to the USA to garner American support for the British cause.

These activities, plus his well-informed writings, led to suggestions that he was a British spy. His 1945 novel *Spy Catchers* was, according to the *Leicester Mercury*, praised as one of the best books on espionage.

CLARE HOLLINGWORTH

Born in 1911 in the village of Knighton, Hollingworth was a journalist and war correspondent. On 31 August 1939, she was in Poland on an assignment from the *Daily Telegraph* to report on growing tensions in Europe.

While driving along the Polish–German border, Hollingworth noticed a massing of German tanks and troops. Realising that she had witnessed a gathering invasion force, she filed her story. Three days later, she was on the phone again, this time to the British Embassy in Warsaw to report the Nazis had invaded Poland. The embassy was unconvinced – so Hollingworth hung her phone out of the window so they could hear the German troops.

Hollingworth was not only one of the first people to witness the outbreak of war, but she was also the first journalist to report it.

OTHER LEICESTERSHIRE LITERARY FIGURES

SUE TOWNSEND The late author of the Adrian Mole books was born and bred in Leicester. A lifelong socialist, Townsend's political beliefs influenced many of her books and plays.

COLIN WILSON Another Leicester writer, Wilson was the author of *The Outsider* and associated with the 'Angry Young Men' movement of the 1960s.

C.P. SNOW, CBE The novelist and physicist was born in Leicester and educated at what is now the University of Leicester.

FREDERICK THORPE Thorpe was the publisher behind Ulverscroft Large Print Books, which were produced to help those with failing eyesight to keep on reading. The name for his publishing house came from the old Augustine priory near his farm in Leicestershire.

JOE ORTON Leicester-born playwright and author whose literary style was best described as 'Ortonesque', so particular were his cynical black comedies. Orton was murdered by his partner Kenneth Halliwell in 1967.

Many famous literary figures have also passed through Leicestershire. SAMUEL JOHNSON, the famous essayist and lexicographer, worked briefly as a teacher at Dixie Grammar School, after he prematurely left Oxford because of debt. However, Johnson's post did not last long and he quit after only four months because he was unable to tolerate the 'boorish' 4th baronet.

Poet laureate PHILIP LARKIN lived in Leicester in the 1940s, when he worked in the University of Leicester's library. While in the city, Larkin wrote thirteen poems. His last address in the city, on Dixon Drive, provided the surname for his friend Kingsley Amis's hero Jim Dixon, the eponymous hero of *Lucky Jim*.

ARTISTS AND CRAFTSPEOPLE

MARY LINWOOD

Born in Birmingham in 1755, Mary Linwood was a famous needlework artist who made Leicester her home. She moved to the town in 1764 when her wine merchant father became bankrupt and her mother opened a boarding school for young ladies. Mary took over the school and continued to run it for the next fifty years. Simultaneously, however, she made a name for herself as an embroidery artist. By the age of 31, Mary was mixing with royalty, exhibiting her work to Queen Charlotte at Windsor Castle.

Over her lifetime Mary produced sixty-four pictures, many of which were full-sized copies of Old Masters. She met most of the crowned heads of Europe and exhibited in Russia, where Catherine the Great tried to buy her whole collection for £40,000. Mary refused, as she wanted her work to stay in England. One piece, however, was purchased: a copy of a painting by the Italian artist Salvator Rosa, which sold for more than the original.

Mary also created her own designs such as 'The Judgment of Cain' and a portrait of Napoleon, whom she met in 1803. Napoleon went on to award Mary the Freedom of Paris.

JOHN FLOWER

Known as 'The Leicester Artist', Flower was a landscape and architectural artist born in Leicester in 1793.

Initially apprenticed to a framework knitter, Flower's talent for drawing was noticed by a local doctor, who gave him art lessons. Mary Linwood eventually became his patron and it was she who arranged for him to study art in London.

On his return to Leicester, Flower began to teach art and paint landscapes. His work was very much concentrated around Leicestershire, although he did branch out to neighbouring counties. In 1826 he published *Views of Ancient Buildings in the Town and County of Leicester*. He remained in Leicester until his death in 1861, in the home he and the architect Henry Goddard designed on Upper Regent Street (now Regent Road).

ERNEST GIMSON

Gimson was born in Leicester in 1864, the son of Josiah Gimson, the owner of the Vulcan Works and founder of Gimson & Co. Ernest was apprenticed to a Leicester architect at the age of 18, but when he attended a lecture on arts and socialism given by William Morris at the Leicester Secular Society, he became inspired.

That night, he talked with Morris until two o'clock in the morning, the beginning of a long-standing association. Once his architectural education was complete, Gimson moved to London, armed with letters of recommendation from Morris. There, he began to develop his own style, using naturalistic details, flowers, animals and natural textures. After travelling, he joined Morris's Society for the Protection of Ancient Buildings and moved to the Cotswolds to found an artisan community, experimenting in furniture design.

Many of Gimson's buildings remain around Leicestershire. They include Inglewood and The White House in Stoneygate, and Lea, Stoneywell and Rockyfield Cottages in Charnwood.

Gimson died in 1919 and was described by the architectural historian Nikolaus Pevsner as 'the greatest of the English architect-designers'.

LOCAL CHARACTERS

In his day, DANIEL LAMBERT was the heaviest man in England – but he didn't start out that way. Until his mid-twenties, Lambert was tall and well-built but not overweight. He swam regularly, even teaching local children, and ate a moderate diet, drinking only water.

Then, for no explicable reason, he began to balloon, until by the age of 35, he had reached 53 stone. Unable to continue in his role as gaoler of Leicester Prison, Lambert briefly moved to London, where he made a living from being 'visited' by gawpers at his house. But he quickly returned home, where he died at the age of 39 after visiting Stamford Races.

JOSEPH MERRICK, nicknamed the Elephant Man, was born in Leicester in 1862, in the slum area of Wharf Street. Joseph was a healthy child until at 21 months growths began to appear on his body – including one that resembled an elephant's trunk across his mouth. Soon after, his mother died and Joseph, rejected by his father, was left to fend for himself. Unable to find employment, he was forced into Leicester Workhouse for three years until in 1884 he joined a freak show.

In London, Frederick Treves, a doctor at the Royal London Hospital, spotted Merrick on his return from a tour of Belgium. Merrick took up residence at the hospital and remained there until he died in 1890.

4

WORK AND WORKING LIFE

MAJOR EMPLOYERS

Leicestershire folk have been employed in a diverse number of industries over the centuries …

QUARRYING

Quarrying was one of Leicestershire's earliest industries. The geology of the county makes it a rich source of rock to this day, with the hard, igneous rocks of north-west Leicestershire especially important.

Stone from Quorn was been quarried for millstones since the Iron Age and the Romans transported it to build Roman Leicester. No wonder the village's name means 'the hill where the millstones are quarried'.

From Roman times, slate was also important to villages like Swithland, which maintained a trade in the material right the way through to the nineteenth century. Swithland slate was converted into roof tiles and, more unusually, gravestones, due to its rough texture and easy carving.

Charnwood's hard igneous rocks were much sought after for whetstones and quernstones, and even today the granite quarries of Bardon Hill, Breedon Hill and Whitwick are an important source of crushed aggregate, which is transported around the country. The pink granite of Mountsorrel has also been prized since the eighteenth century.

FARMING

As with most places, agriculture was a mainstay of the Leicestershire economy up until the Industrial Revolution. Sheep and cattle were the most common commodities, as Leicestershire's heavy clay soils are still hard work for growing crops.

After 1650, livestock farming became more common as grain prices fell and the profits for wool and dairy began to rise. However, British livestock, like the now nearly extinct Forest sheep of Charnwood, were generally small and not known for the quality of their meat.

Then, in the eighteenth century, an agricultural revolution occurred in Leicestershire. Farmer Robert Bakewell of Dishley near Loughborough began to pioneer selective breeding. His experiments resulted in two new types of livestock: Longwool sheep and Longhorn cattle. Both were the cornerstones for the future of meat and wool across Leicestershire and England. Longwool sheep, now a heritage breed and the ancestor of many later breeds such as the English Leicester, the Border Leicester, Bluefaced Leicester, Scotch Mule and Welsh Halfbred, produced excellent wool and mutton, while Longhorn cattle are esteemed even today for their meat and milk.

THE WOOL AND HOSIERY INDUSTRY

Even before Robert Bakewell's agricultural breakthrough, wool was a major part of Leicestershire's economy, from the Middle Ages onwards. Shepshed was one village noted for its sheep farming and wool production. Indeed, its name may well mean 'hill where sheep graze'.

Well Yard on Forest Street was once known as the 'Wool Yard'. This was the place where merchants gathered to buy Shepshed wool. Buyers would come from as far afield as Bradford and the abbey that owned the village and its farmland had permission to sell to merchants from Flanders. Shepshed's role in the wool trade remained important up until the early nineteenth century.

But agriculture never paid well and so it became common to supplement the farm labouring families' incomes with hand-knitting. This cottage industry dominated in the south and east of Leicestershire until the end of the seventeenth century.

In the Tudor era, two changes occurred. First, men's fashion changed when the doublet and hose replaced the long robes of the medieval period. This meant the legs were now on show, making the stocking a fashion item in its own right, rather than just an undergarment.

The second change was the invention of the first stocking frame in 1589 by William Lee of Calverton, near Nottingham. By 1640, the stocking frame had reached Leicestershire when William Iliffe of Hinckley set one up in his own house for £60. Iliffe started a trend and soon stocking workers across the county were working from home on rented frames. In 1720, Daniel Defoe noted:

> Leicester is an ancient, large and populous town ... they have considerable manufacture carried on here and in several of the market towns round for weaving stockings by frames and one would scarce think it possible so small an article of trade could employ such multitudes of people as it does; for the whole county seems to be employ'd in it.

By the seventeenth century, the stocking frame was part of the working life of country stocking knitters too and people adapted their homes to accommodate the industry. Long windows were added to existing workrooms or new rooms were built to allow the plentiful light required for the craft.

By 1753 there were 1,000 frames in Shepshed alone. In 1801, out of a population of 1,628, 1,493 people were involved in the hosiery trade. Stockingers worked long hours: approximately seventy per week, condensed into a five-day period.

By the nineteenth century, Leicestershire, along with Derbyshire and Nottinghamshire, was the centre of the British hosiery industry. By 1832, Leicestershire was the dominant county, holding the majority of knitting frames.

The invention of the wide frame brought about another revolution, increasing productivity. But the new frames were too large for homes. So, the mid nineteenth century marked the transition from home knitting to factory work.

THE LUDDITES

The advent of factory work was not well received by the knitters themselves. More efficient, large-scale production meant fewer workers were required.

Angry and afraid over the loss of their livelihoods, gangs of disgruntled workers began breaking into the new factories and destroying the machines. They became known as 'Luddites', after an Anstey man named Ned Ludd who lived in the late eighteenth century.

Ned was reputedly a simple boy and a target of local bullies. One day, while hiding from his tormentors in a knitter's cottage, Ned smashed a frame in anger. From then onwards, if something got broken, it was common to say 'Ned Ludd's been at it again'.

Across the country, particularly Nottinghamshire, Lancashire and Leicestershire, angry workers who had been replaced by machinery took sledgehammers to the looms. Naturally, this threw the establishment into a panic. With the French Revolution still fresh in their minds, harsh penalties were put in place to attempt to curb this industrial sabotage, political dissent and social unrest – and so machine-breaking was declared a capital crime.

But the Luddites continued undeterred, warning factory owners of their intent to destroy with letters signed 'Ned Ludd'.

In June 1816, one particular group were apprehended for machine-breaking in the Loughborough factory of a Mr Heathcote – a night's work that ultimately cost them their lives.

First to be captured was James Towle, a stocking knitter. James was tried at the Leicester Assizes in August 1816 and hanged, staunchly refusing to name his accomplices.

In January 1817, James Blackburn, another stockinger, was caught poaching. Blackburn injured the gamekeeper who caught him, and needed to bargain for his life. So, to literally save his own neck, he turned King's evidence, admitted he had been part of the Loughborough raid and named his accomplices.

On 17 April 1817, six of those men – William Withers, Thomas Savage, John Amos, Joshua Mitchell, John Crowther and William Towle, also known as Rodney (James Towle's younger brother) – were hanged at noon at Leicester Prison. A sympathetic crowd of 15,000 gathered to watch them die, singing hymns as a show of solidarity as the men walked to the gallows.

CORAH & SONS

Hosiery factories had existed in Leicestershire since the eighteenth century. Donisthorpe Mill in Leicester is one of the oldest mills in the East Midlands, manufacturing since the 1730s.

The most famous Leicestershire hosiery firm was Corah's. Over its 150-year lifespan, the company employed thousands of Leicester people at its St Margaret's Works, with other branches countrywide, supplying companies such as Marks and Spencer.

The company also had a reputation for benevolence towards its employees – especially in the early twentieth century. Older workers were retained until they wished to retire, and the company encouraged sports, having its own bowling, skittles, cricket and football teams, as well inviting employees to an annual dinner.

Outside Leicester, Anstey, Earl Shilton and Kegworth were all key hosiery towns. Kegworth's stocking makers were so skilful that they supplied British and foreign royalty. Melton Mowbray also became famous for its 'Melton Cloth', a tightly woven, dense-piled woollen material first recorded in 1823. The cloth was used to make sailor's coats and donkey jackets and, in North America, loggers' jackets.

But it was not only wool that was worked in Leicestershire. In 1809, the 'Twisted Lace Machine' found its way to Loughborough. The machine allowed for fine, lace-like work to be mass-produced. So famous did the town become for its mittens that the machine was often referred to as 'the Loughborough Machine'.

THE SHOE INDUSTRY

Leather, as a by-product of cattle farming, was readily available in Leicestershire. But that wasn't the reason that Leicestershire became a major shoe manufacturer. In 1853, a Leicester shoemaker called Thomas Crick received the letters patent for an invention that would revolutionize the manufacture of boots and shoes. Crick had invented a riveting machine that fastened the uppers and soles of footwear together using 'tacks, rivets or sprigs' instead of stitches.

Crick's innovation allowed shoe manufacture to become the second biggest industry in Leicestershire. His invention increased the productivity and profitability of shoemaking. In 1851, there were 1,393 people employed in making boots and shoes in Leicester. By 1861, there were 2,741, an increase that bucked the trend for the country as a whole, which had seen a drop in numbers employed in the industry.

Shoemaking spread about the county. By 1863, Anstey had its first registered 'boot and shoe manufacturer' supplied by the village's leather industry. Earl Shilton was also a major shoe producer and established large factories such as Ortons, Eatoughs and E. Pinchess & Co. Ltd. Leicester itself saw the establishment of firms such as Freeman, Hardy and Willis and Oliver's, which in its day was the largest retailer of boots and shoes in the world.

COAL MINING

Coal had always been mined in Leicestershire, particularly in the 10-mile-square area in the north-west around Coleorton and Swannington.

In the Middle Ages, there were small pits around Swannington, Worthington, Staunton Harold, and Swadlincote. In the fifteenth century, Leicester Abbey also held an interest in mines at Oakthorpe.

The coal in these areas was generally on the surface. In 1572, it is recorded that gangs of fifteen to twenty men from Swannington were paid a shilling for every 1–2 tons of coal they gathered.

Where there were mines, they were not deep. At Coleorton, evidence from the late fifteenth century shows shafts only extended 30m below the surface.

The richer seams of coal lay deeper and so out of reach – until the Industrial Revolution. Then, in 1824, a mining engineer called William Stenson decided to try and sink a shaft on farmland near Whitwick. He struck lucky and found coal.

Mining exploded in the north-west of Leicestershire. By 1880, there were twenty-six pits centred around Whitwick, Bardon Hill, Ashby de la Zouch, Burton, Woodville, Ibstock, Bagworth, Coleorton, Snibston and Coalville.

But by the late twentieth century, mining began to die in Leicestershire. Thorntree Drift and Reservoir closed in the late 1940s and the 1960s saw the closure of a further eight collieries. By the end of the late 1980s, only one pit remained, Bagworth Colliery, which only survived until 1991.

In 1990, coal mining in Leicestershire underwent a brief renaissance with the Asfordby Super Pit in the Vale of Belvoir. But in 1997, it too was closed down due to 'unsurmountable geological problems' caused by volcanic rocks putting too much pressure on the underlying coal seams.

THE WHITWICK COLLIERY DISASTER

Mining was fraught with danger and accidents were common. In Leicestershire alone, 355 men are recorded as losing their lives in the county's pits. So, it is no surprise that miners were a superstitious bunch. The cry of the golden plover, in particular, was believed to warn of impending calamity in the pits.

The worst mining disaster in Leicestershire history occurred in 1898 at the Whitwick Colliery. Forty-two men went down number five shaft that night. Only seven returned alive.

The disaster was sparked by a gob fire, an underground blaze of disused material that became out of control. The flames consumed the wooden support timbers of the shaft roof, bringing about its collapse and raining fire down upon the miners trapped within.

As news of the disaster spread, crowds gathered, hoping for the best – yet fearing the worst. Witnesses described how women sobbed 'as though their hearts were going to break'. A reporter from the *Mercury* was told by one of the rescue workers, 'They're all dead, my lad. I have worked in the pit seventy years and I know.'

Of the thirty-five men killed, only nine bodies were returned to the surface. Those bodies that were found were discovered huddled together with their arms around each other's necks. Many of the men's features were unrecognisable and they could only be identified by the personal possessions found in their pockets.

The first body brought to the surface was that of Charles Clamp, who had managed to scramble to safety but then doubled back to help his comrades. The disaster's youngest victim was John Albert Gee of Thringstone. He was just 13 years old. When thick smoke was noticed coming from the shaft, John had been sent down the pit by the mine's deputy to order the men out.

PLANES, TRAINS, CRANES, IRON AND AUTOMOBILES

Engineering was, and still is, another major Leicestershire employer. The Asfordby Hill Steel Works, near Melton Mowbray, were constructed in 1878, although they did not begin working until 1881. Today, the works are still going strong.

Initially owned by the Holwell Iron Company, the steel works were originally built to smelt iron. Later, a foundry was added so that iron could also be cast.

But as pig iron from abroad became cheaper in the 1950s and '60s, the company began to decline as an iron-smelting plant. So Ashfordby branched out into steel manufacturing. It is now responsible for producing most of the drain covers in the UK. In 1996, it was also assigned the task of melting down a large number of weapons handed in to Leicestershire police as part of an amnesty.

Herbert Morris Ltd was established in 1884 and in 1897 moved its base to the Empress Works in Loughborough. The firm became famous for its cranes and joists, which it exported across the globe, to places as varied as New Jersey and Korea. Its largest ever construct weighed 400 tons.

The firm closed in Loughborough in 2010 when its then owner, Finnish company Konecranes, moved operations to Scotland.

Trains, planes and automobiles have all been made in Leicestershire. Sports-car maker Noble Automotive originally established itself in Barwell. The reborn Triumph Motorcycles built its factory in Hinckley in 1988 and began producing its first new motorcycles in 1991. The Falcon Works in Loughborough began making turbines for steam locomotives and trams in

1865, before branching out into aircraft during the First World War. From then on, the works continued to make and mend planes, providing a major service in the Second World War. Today, Mallory Park near Kirkby Mallory and Bruntingthorpe Aerodrome continue this tradition, providing testing facilities for automotive and aerospace engineers.

Not all of Leicestershire's engineering ventures were a success. In the early nineteenth century, the earls of Moira, Ireland, built an industrial village named after them near Coalville, on the banks of the Ashby de la Zouch Canal. The centre of the village's industry was a blast furnace erected in 1805. But the venture was not a success. Not only was the local ironstone of poor quality but the furnace didn't work effectively. It was abandoned in 1811 but survived because it was so little used – which is why the Moira Furnace is one of the few surviving furnaces of this era and is now a scheduled ancient monument.

CRAFTS

BELL FOUNDING

Leicestershire's earliest major bell founder was Johannes de Stafford, who is believed to have had a foundry in Leicester in the late fourteenth century. De Stafford was famed for his high-quality bells, which were installed in local churches at Aylestone, Beeby, Great Glen, Little Dalby, Loddington, Ratby, Shenton and Thrussington. De Stafford's foundry also cast a large bell for York Minster in 1371.

In his day, de Stafford was probably only one of many bell founders in England. Today, Leicestershire has one of the only two bell-founding businesses left in the country. John Taylor & Co. established themselves in Loughborough in 1839. Their first commission was the recasting of bells for a local church. But by 1881, they had moved on to bigger things, namely 'Great Paul' in St Paul's Cathedral. The bell was their largest commission and, at 16 tons, it is still the largest bell in England.

Today, Taylor's is the world's largest functioning bell foundry and regularly casts new bells for churches – including York Minster.

STAINED GLASS

Norman and Underwood are the oldest independent family company in Leicester. The company began life in 1825 as a general plumbers and glaziers, but after several years the firm began to specialise in glass. In 1866, the company received its first and largest commission: to glaze the roof of St Pancras Station.

Work on many major churches and historic buildings followed, including Salisbury Cathedral, Windsor Castle, Westminster Abbey, Chatsworth House and Hampton Court.

The company also restore historic windows. One of their major projects was the restoration of St Ethelburga's, the historic church in Bishopsgate damaged by an IRA bomb in 1993.

POTTERY

Measham has been an area of clay extraction since the Middle Ages. From the nineteenth century it has also been the home of the famous Measham Ware – a type of pottery covered with a dark brown glaze and painted with white clay flowers and mottos such as 'Home is Best' and 'Friendship'.

Measham Ware was particularly associated with canal boats, as passing hauliers would order their pots from the High Street shop of Mrs Annie Bonas. Mrs Bonas commissioned the pottery from manufacturers in Church Gresley and Woodville in Derbyshire. She would hold the finished items for the hauliers to collect on their return journey through Measham.

Teapots were the most popular form of Measham Ware. They were often ordered by seasonal farmworkers from Norfolk and Suffolk who worked at the maltings of Burton upon Trent, who then took the pots home as gifts for friends and family.

TRANSPORT

THE RAILWAY

William Stenson was not only the father of coal mining in Leicestershire but arguably the godfather of its railway. Stenson recognised the potential of the fledgling transport system to his burgeoning industry and quickly sought out partners.

Joining with local landowner John Ellis and Ellis's friend George Stephenson, the designer of Stephenson's Rocket, Stenson formed the Leicester and Swannington Railway (L&S). Stephenson's son Robert became the railway's chief engineer.

Sixteen miles of track were built in two stages, with the first section of the line running from Leicester to Bagworth opening in July 1832. The remainder was completed by 1836. The tunnel built by Stephenson at Glenfield near the line's first station, was, at 1 mile 36 yards long, for a time the world's longest railway tunnel. As well as being the first railway in Leicestershire, the Leicester to Swannington Railway was the first in the Midlands and, according to the Swannington Heritage Trust, only the fifth line in the world to be authorised and built.

THE CANAL

Before the railway, it was the canal that initiated Leicester's industrial growth.

The Grand Union Canal came to Leicestershire in the late eighteenth century, bringing, in the words of the *Leicester Guardian*, 'extensive advantages to town and country'. Coal was the principal reason for its construction as the canal connected Leicestershire with nearby Derbyshire coalfields.

Foxton Locks were part of this canal system and boasted a particularly ingenious innovation. The natural incline of the land at the locks slowed down the canal boats, so that it took them an hour to pass through. This was annoyingly inefficient. So, between 1897 and 1900, an inclined plane was built to speed up the passage through Foxton's ten locks. Instead of passing through each lock, the barges were loaded into a cradle and lifted up the hillside, cutting the journey time to ten minutes.

WORKING PEOPLE

LIFE ON THE LAND

Life for a farmworker in Leicestershire was no bucolic dream. Discipline was strict. Some could even say it represented a form of paid bondage because of the rules imposed on workers – and the penalties for breaking them.

Even into the early twentieth century it was customary to refer to the farmer as 'master'. This was more than just a title of deference, for labourers' employers literally had control of their lives for the tenure of their employment. This control even extended to their supposed free time.

In 1869, two young labourers were arrested and taken before Lutterworth magistrates. Their 'crime' had been to go out after work without asking their employer's permission. The labourers were ordered to apologise to their employer and pay a fine of seven shillings each – or face fourteen days in prison!

Farmers and their labourers would sign a contract of employment upon their hiring. Before the 1867 Master and Servant Act, any labourer who broke this contract by leaving prematurely was liable to be imprisoned. On the other hand, an employer who let his hireling go before time was only fined.

So it is little wonder that the town was a lure, perhaps seen as offering a freer or more prosperous life.

THE POOR LAW

In times of boom, it was easy to get a job. But when work dried up, as it did at various times in early nineteenth-century Leicestershire, workers would be laid off without pay – very much like the zero contract workers of today.

No work meant no money. And that left the unemployed only two choices if they could not find alternative work: the parish or the poorhouse.

Initially, if the parish deemed you to be 'worthy', you would be maintained in your home, by being allowed 'out relief': vouchers, food and the basic necessities of life. But if for any reason you were branded as part of the 'unworthy poor', your only choice was the workhouse.

The Poor Law Amendment Act of 1834 allowed parishes in England and Wales to form into Poor Law Unions. With the formation of the Leicester Poor Law Union in June 1836, the practice of 'out relief' began to be phased out and from 1837 the able-bodied poor were also required to enter the workhouse.

However, this rule change corresponded with a depression in the hosiery industry, which increased the number of people throwing themselves on the mercy of the parish. So, in Leicester at least, out relief remained. During the depression of 1841–42, 5,000 people in Leicester claimed out relief. During this time, an average of 25 per cent of workhouse residents were skilled workers who, through no fault of their own, had been left without work.

Besides Leicester, there were workhouses at Ashby de la Zouch, Barrow upon Soar, Billesdon, Blaby, Hinckley, Loughborough, Lutterworth, Market Bosworth, Market Harborough and Melton Mowbray.

Before they became the responsibility of the borough, workhouses were little more than glorified sweatshops, run by private contractors who used the inmates as cheap labour for their own businesses. In Leicester in 1720, at a workhouse in St Martin's parish, inmates were required to work twelve hours a day, summer and winter, at spinning or stockmaking.

Even after the establishment of union workhouses, things were little better. At Hinckley, the workhouse was known as 'The Bastille', with some inmates chained, accidentally poisoned or declared lunatics.

But not every workhouse regime was harsh. In the early twentieth century, the governor of Mountsorrel workhouse assessed the talents and attributes of inmates, allocating them work suitable to their skill set.

SLUM LIFE

Having a job didn't guarantee you a decent standard of living. Many of Leicestershire's factory workers called the slums home. These badly built, basic residences were constructed as quickly and cheaply as possible in order to profit from the flood of factory workers into Leicestershire's towns in the 1800s.

Leicester city centre was riddled with slums, with the area around Charles Street and what is now the ring road a warren of unsanitary homes for the working poor. Notorious areas included Palmerston Street, Carley Street, Baker Street and Wharf Street – the last area to be cleared.

Houses were based around a cobbled central yard. Unheated and without independent supplies of water, what facilities there were were shared. Communal toilets often overspilled – providing the perfect breeding ground for disease.

In 1871, at the peak of Leicester's prosperity when industrialisation had made it one of the richest cities in the world, it was estimated that one in four children died of diarrhoea before their first birthday. This placed infant mortality in Leicester's slums at twice the national average.

Some claimed that the unrelenting harshness of the slums drove its residents to depravity. In the 1920s, Councillor Grimsley, a member of the Leicester borough and a Methodist minister, claimed many slum women had taken to drinking methylated spirits laced with lemon juice to blot out the misery of their existence, harming both unborn and living children with their negligence.

But many felt statements like this were a way of displacing some of the blame for the dangers of life in the slums. Union leader Mary Bell Richards maintained that despite the hardships of their daily life, slum women were decent and hardworking and were determined to make the best of things for themselves and their children.

Slum clearance began after the First World War with the drive for 'homes fit for heroes'. At first modernisation was attempted, but it soon became clear that it was better to clear away the slums altogether. In 1929, the Leicester Corporation gave the green light to demolition and in 1930 the bulldozers moved in and the residents moved out as the first slums in Leicester were destroyed. The former residents of these slums, on Green and Sandacre Streets, were moved to smart new homes on the newly constructed Talby estate.

Other Leicestershire towns followed suit, with Hinckley beginning its slum clearance later in the decade. But it was not until the 1950s that Leicestershire was slum-free.

INDUSTRIAL UNREST

It is a mistake to think that Leicestershire people accepted the hardships of working life without complaint – even if they weren't directly affected. In 1842, the people of Leicester rose up and rioted against the guardians of the workhouses, who were forcing those still living off the parish in their own homes to break stone.

Nor was this the only protest of those times.

THOMAS COOPER AND THE CHARTISTS

Thomas Cooper was a poet and leading member of the Chartist movement, an organisation that believed in universal suffrage and worker's rights. Cooper was born in Leicester on 20 March 1805. By trade a shoemaker, he self-educated himself, becoming a teacher before moving into journalism.

After cutting his journalistic teeth in London and Lincoln, in 1840 Cooper returned home and joined the staff of the *Leicestershire Mercury*. By this time he was a dedicated Chartist and determined to make Leicester a Chartist stronghold.

While at the *Mercury*, Cooper published his own Chartist journal, *The Commonwealthman*, and became a leading lecturer for the movement. He also helped organise strikes in Leicestershire that expressed part of the general wave of discontent in the northern counties, brought about by hunger and mass unemployment that arose during the summer of 1842.

Cooper organised miners' strikes over low wages and rallied disgruntled hosiery workers, who were working only half a week but still paying their employers full rent for their frames. The workers took to the streets of Leicester with banners and flags, calling for others to join them. Local magistrates, alarmed by the swelling crowds, swore in special constables to be on standby.

On 19 August, hundreds of strikers were listening to speakers at Humberstone Gate when they were advised by the speakers to arm themselves and hurry to Loughborough to support protesters under attack from the authorities.

But the police pursued them and turned them off the road at Mowmacre Hill just outside the city. Although the yeomanry charged at the strikers, there was no blood spilled during the 'battle', although it did have the effect of ending the strikes – on this occasion.

On 26 August 1842, Thomas Cooper was arrested at his home at Church Gate, Leicester, and put on trial in Stafford for his part in riots in the Staffordshire Potteries. He was sentenced to two years in prison. While inside, Cooper wrote *The Purgatory of Suicides*, a 944-stanza poem discussing the dawning of an age of freedom and equality.

That was not the only year of disputing hosiery workers:

- In 1787, John Coltman and Joseph Whetstone tried to introduce a steam stocking-making machine in Leicester. Local workers were enraged at the threat to their livelihood and rioted for a week, storming the home of the owners and wrecking the machine.
- In 1824 and 1826 in Hinckley strikes by framework knitters were so disorderly that the army had to be called in to manage the strikers.
- In 1859, 130 hosiery workers at Messrs Homer and Everard of Earl Shilton withdrew their labour and called upon workers from Leicestershire, Derbyshire and Nottinghamshire to join them.

THE GENERAL STRIKE

Mass unemployment after the First World War led to further industrial unrest in the 1920s. In 1921, the Leicester unemployed rioted around the clock tower in the city centre. Further dissent followed in 1926, when low wages and poor working conditions in the mining industry led to the General Strike.

Over 7,000 people from various trade unions joined the strike – the majority being railway workers. In Dunton Bassett near Harborough, one of the village's special constables was called upon to guard the local railway tunnel from striking railwaymen, who were believed to be planning to damage the tunnel to prevent coal being transported by train. The constable, who knew many of the men, did not believe they would damage railway property and sympathised with their cause. So, he refused. As a result, he was ordered to give up his badge and resign.

THE 1984–5 MINERS' STRIKE

In Leicestershire in the mid-1980s there were 2,500 miners, but only thirty chose to strike during the Miners' Strike. While their colleagues ignored the decision of the National Union of Mineworkers to strike, 'The Dirty Thirty' stood true to the cause, despite the financial hardship and peer pressure. Their leader was

Malcolm Pinnegar, who believed Leicestershire miners should support mining comrades around the country who were fighting for their jobs.

They were right. By the end of the 1980s, most of Leicestershire's pits were closed.

INDUSTRIAL REDEVELOPMENT

Many of Leicestershire's old industries and industrial sites are now defunct and closed. However, they have morphed into a new way for Leicestershire residents to make a living. The following are just a couple of examples.

WIGSTON FRAMEWORK KNITTERS MUSEUM

Once a seventeenth-century master hosier's house, complete with its frame shop in the garden, the Wigston Framework Knitters Museum perfectly preserves the living and working conditions of Leicestershire's cottage hosiers. The museum is unique in that it was still in use as a hosier's place of work and residence until 1952 when the last resident, Edgar Carter, died – leaving in situ his eight hand frames and all the tools of his trade.

ABBEY PUMPING STATION

Opened in 1891, the Abbey Pumping Station was Leicester's state-of-the-art sewerage works. The building's elegant architecture, like many of its type, belied its function. So too did its decorative beam engines.

The sewerage works closed in 1964. But the pumping station lives on – as a museum of science and technology. The beam engines also remain in full working order.

5

CRIME AND PUNISHMENT

PRISONS

LOCK-UPS

Most Leicestershire towns and villages had small buildings for holding petty criminals or those awaiting transfer to the county gaols. Known as 'blind houses', 'round houses' or lock-ups, they were little more than windowless stone sheds. Examples still remain at Barrow upon Soar, Breedon on the Hill, Castle Donington, Packington and Worthington.

THE OLD COUNTY GAOL

The county gaol was always situated in the principal town of Leicestershire – Leicester. However, before 1309, Leicester criminals were transported to Warwick gaol after conviction. The only place in Leicester to house prisoners was the Earl's gaol, which was probably located in the dungeons of Leicester Castle.

This all changed in August 1309 when Leicestershire's first, dedicated county gaol opened. According to Charles James Billson, Edward I ordered in 1301 that 'for the convenience of the inhabitants of Leicestershire ... a public prison should be made in the town of Leicester'. For this reason, this original county gaol was also known as 'The King's Prison'.

The county goal underwent several incarnations on Leicester's Highcross Street. The final gaol built on the site was constructed in the early 1790s. This gaol's first inmate was its architect, George

Moneypenny, who was committed there between 1792 and 1793 for debt!

The prison had a fearsome reputation, described by one convict as 'hell on earth'. In the mid-nineteenth century, it ran a separatist regime where prisoners were kept in isolation to prevent them from 'polluting' their fellow prisoners further.

In 1828, the county gaol moved to the newly constructed prison on Welford Road. The gaol on Highcross Street was then downgraded to Leicester's town prison, which it remained until its final demolition in 1897.

WELFORD ROAD PRISON

The prison was built in 1825 and opened in 1828 because of the inadequacy of the old county gaol. It covered 3 acres and was built to conform to new standards, designed to ensure that 'the security and comfort of the prisoners are specially regarded'.

The exterior of the prison looks like a medieval castle – which even today causes many unwitting tourists to queue outside in the mistaken belief it is Leicester Castle. Perhaps this is why, in the event of the prison closing, Leicester City Council has considered the option of converting the prison into a hotel!

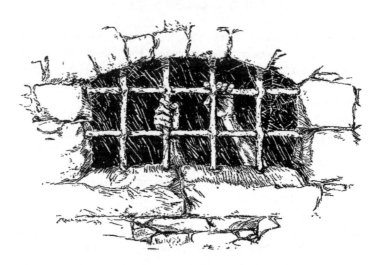

Executions once took place outside Welford Road Prison on a temporary drop that was erected in front of the turreted entrance. The first hangings at the newly built prison took place on 20 April 1829, when three men were hanged for horse stealing.

LEICESTER'S BRIDEWELL PRISONS

A bridewell was a sixteenth-century prison for petty criminals, based on the pattern of the original Bridewell in London.

In the nineteenth century, Leicester somewhat confusingly had two bridewells. One, which opened in 1830, stood near the location of the old county gaol on Highcross Street. This bridewell was known as the House of Correction or the Leicester Bridewell. The County Bridewell, on the other hand, was built in 1804. It stood at the lower end of Oxford Street, near to Leicester Royal Infirmary. It was equipped for hard labour, with prisoners working treadmills to grind corn, some for use within the gaol, while the rest was sold to the public.

PRISON BREAKS

Perhaps the most daring prison break in Leicestershire's history was that of highwayman William 'Swift Nick' Nevison.

Born to a respectable family, probably in Pontefract in 1639, young Nevison was a bit of a lad – until he stepped over the line into crime, stealing money and a horse to make a new life in London.

After a stint in the army, Nevison began his career on the road, adopting the façade of a gentleman highwayman. He was chivalrous to women and kind to the poor. He even tried to return to the straight and narrow after he returned home to make up with his father – only to return to his bad ways after the old man's death.

It was during this time that Nevison was caught in Leicestershire and committed to Leicester Gaol. Due to his notoriety, Swift Nick was well secured and closely guarded. Escape looked unlikely. But he had a plan.

First, he feigned illness and summoned a group of trusted friends, one of whom was a 'doctor'. This gentleman explained to the gaoler that Nevison had a 'pestilential fever' and needed fresh air – or the whole gaol would be infected. Nevison was duly unfettered and given his own room. A nurse and doctor visited him twice a day – while the fearful goalers gave him a wide berth!

This was just as Nevison had planned. While unattended, the doctor painted Nick with blue plague spots and the fake patient was then dosed up to appear lifeless. When he came to inspect the body, one glimpse of the spots was enough for the goaler, who was more than happy to see the infectious corpse out of his prison.

So Swift Nick escaped Leicester Gaol in a coffin and for a while everyone did indeed believe he was dead – until his 'ghost' began 'haunting' the roads of Leicestershire. It wasn't long before it dawned on the authorities that Swift Nick wasn't quite so dead after all.

ESCAPE FROM THE OLD BOROUGH GAOL

In August 1867, 25-year-old jewel thief John McCarty was serving seven years in the gaol on Highcross Street. The prison was undergoing modification at the time, necessitating the demolition of part of the boundary wall.

One day, while exercising under guard, McCarty took his chance, dodging the warders and escaping through the gap in the wall. Dropping down into the street below, he was quickly away. The guards within the prison, unable to leave their prisoners for fear of other escapes through the prison's breached defences, could only blow their whistles to sound the alarm.

McCarty managed to make it as far as the canal at Fleckney before the police caught up with him. But he didn't give up and tried to escape once again on the way back to Leicester, where he was finally, safely locked up.

WELFORD ROAD PRISON'S ONLY ESCAPEE

On 18 December 1953, renowned safe blower Albert Hattersley became Welford Road's only known escapee. Absconding through a skylight in the prison workshop, Hattersley scaled the prison wall and then made the drop into the governor's garden – and freedom!

Hattersley had hoped the soft ground would break his fall. He was wrong. He broke his ankle so badly that part of the bone was left sticking out. But he still managed to get away from the prison – until the following day at least, when he was recaptured. Who knows, maybe with a sound ankle, he could have made good his escape?

GARTREE PRISON

The name of Gartree or *Gore Tree* commemorated the oak tree that marked the ancient meeting place of the elders of the Gartree Hundred. Here, they held a court between 1458 and 1750. The open air apparently ensured the proceedings were free from the influence of the malign spirits of buildings!

The grove is now gone and in its place stands Gartree Prison. Opened in 1965, it has played host to such infamous inmates as Charles Bronson, Reggie Kray, Ian Brady and Fred West.

In December 1987, the prison was the site of a dramatic and unique breakout. Lifer Sydney Draper and gangland boss John Kendall, who was serving eight years, were lifted out of the prison yard in spectacular fashion by a stolen helicopter. Kendall was recaptured after ten days but murderer Draper remained at large for another thirteen months.

THE ASSIZES

The assizes were periodic courts held around English counties until 1972, when they were replaced with the county court system. They dealt with the most serious crimes.

The Great Hall of Leicester Castle was used for Leicestershire's assizes from 1273 until 1888, when it became the location of the county court until its closure in 1990.

Its 800 years gives it one of the longest-running records of court usage in England – beaten only by the court at Oakham Castle, which was in use from 1229 and is still occasionally used as a courtroom today.

PUNISHMENTS

HANGING PLACES IN LEICESTERSHIRE

The major execution sites in Leicestershire were:

The Danes Hill Tollgate on Hinckley Road, Leicester. **Red Hill,** near Belgrave. **Infirmary Square,** near to Leicester Prison, which was overlooked by Leicester Infirmary, where patients were allowed to watch the hangings. **Gallowtree Gate.** Today, Gallowtree Gate can be found at the bottom of London Road at the heart of Leicester's city centre. The name originates further out of town, to the south, at the junction of what is now London Road and Evington Road – the place where the gallows were erected.

ALTERNATIVE PUNISHMENTS

The cucking stool seems to have been a Leicestershire favourite for dealing with disorderly women, scolds and dishonest tradesmen. The stool was in fact a chair, in which the unfortunate person was confined. Therein, they were conveyed through the streets until their journey's end – which was often a wet one! In Loughborough, the favourite culmination to a journey in the cucking stool was a dunking in the river, near to Cotes Mill.

Assize records from Leicester in June 1654 detail the sort of incidents that merited such public humiliation. A Thomas Goadby laid a complaint against Ann Rawlins, a Leicester widow who apparently harangued both him and a Mrs Clarke in the street. Mrs Rawlins cast aspersions of the worst kind – and in the ripest language – upon the character of Mrs Clarke's husband. She was found guilty and sentenced to the cucking stool.

It seems a great many people took to insulting Mrs Clarke because at the same assizes, she accused yet another woman of verbally abusing her – this time the wife of one Richard Pole. But the justices of assize seemed to think nothing of this strange coincidence – sentencing the unfortunate Mrs Pole to the same humiliating punishment.

LOCAL LAWMEN

FREDERICK GOODYER

Leicester Police Force was established in 1836 under Frederick Goodyer, one of the very first police officers in Sir Robert Peel's new Metropolitan Police Force. After three years heading Leicester Borough Police, Goodyer became Chief Constable of the newly formed Leicestershire County Police Force.

FRANCIS 'TANKY' SMITH

Francis 'Tanky' Smith was a celebrated detective inspector with Leicester police for twenty-four years. He and his partner, Tommy 'Black Tommy' Haynes, joined up in 1840 as the fledgling force's first detectives. Wearing disguises, the pair infiltrated local criminal gangs to collect evidence for convictions. Their high arrest records made them the town's most successful officers.

In 1862, Tanky dealt with his most famous case: the Winstanley affair. Local squire and the High Sheriff of Leicestershire, Mr James Beaumont Winstanley, had mysteriously disappeared and Tanky was tasked with tracking him down. The trail took the detective to the Continent and ended in Germany, where the High Sheriff was found drowned.

Tanky spent his £1,000 reward from the case on a row of houses on London Road. Designed by his architect son, the terrace became known as Top Hat Terrace from the carvings of Tanky wearing his police top hat – and the variety of disguises he adopted in his work.

In 1863, citing 'failing eyesight and bodily strength', Tanky retired from the force. Retirement, however brief, obviously had restorative powers, for almost immediately he set himself up as Leicester's first private detective.

THE LAUGHING POLICEMAN

PC John William 'Tubby' Stephens was equally famous as Tanky Smith – but for different reasons. PC Stephens was a popular and well-loved Leicester bobby who served for twenty-two years – despite his considerable girth. At his death in 1908 at only 48, Tubby weighed 23 stone and 3lbs and was believed to be England's heaviest policeman. An estimated 10,000 people turned out to pay their respects on the day of his funeral, lining the route from his house to Welford Road Cemetery.

Tubby is said to be the inspiration behind the song 'The Laughing Policeman' because of his jolly, good-humoured nature.

JOHN MARRIOTT

In 1962, local tailor John Marriott began his service as a Leicestershire special constable, patrolling the Belgrave and Beaumont Leys areas.

In 1982, he was awarded a long service medal, but his work with Leicestershire Police did not end there. After a stint as a truancy officer, in 2000 John returned to Leicestershire Police as a Police Support Volunteer, monitoring CCTV footage from around Leicestershire at Melton police station every Wednesday morning. John was still going strong at 85!

EARLY GANGS

THE DE FOLVILLES

John de Folville, Lord of Ashby Folville, had seven sons. After his death in 1310, his eldest son, John, took over the estate. But his other six sons formed a notorious medieval gang that terrorised Leicestershire throughout the 1320s and 1330s.

The gang's first crime is recorded by Henry of Knighton. On 29 January 1326, a Master Roger Bellers was found murdered near Rearsby. His death was laid squarely at the door of 'one Eustace de Folville and his brothers'.

Bellers was a greedy fellow, apparently guilty of persecuting and threatening the de Folvilles, as well as many of his other neighbours. So, his murder may have been tolerated, if not secretly well received by locals. The de Folvilles, however, were still outlawed.

However, in 1329 they were pardoned by the king on the condition they fought for him. This period of reconciliation with authority did not last. While in the garrison at Leicester, the gang robbed the town burgesses. In 1330, the pardon was revoked.

The de Folvilles quickly became a public nuisance, committing more murders and robberies. By 1331, they were at risk of further censure by the law. To forestall this, Richard de Folville, 'a wild and daring man and prone to acts of violence', who was also the rector of Teigh, kidnapped the king's justice Richard de Willoughby as he travelled to Grantham.

Willoughby was only released after he paid his kidnappers 90 marks and swore an oath to 'comply with their instructions' – which was presumably to protect them from outlawry.

Eustace de Folville, the eldest of the gang, managed to elude justice, dying a natural death in 1347 having served the king in the Hundred Years' War. Richard did not fare so well. In 1340, justice finally caught up with him as the ruthless rector sought sanctuary in his own church with two other gang members. A stand-off between the criminals and their pursuers occurred, with the Reverend de Folville killing one man with his bow before he was eventually dragged from the church and beheaded.

Because he was a priest, Richard's death was deemed unlawful, so his killers had to do penance by praying for forgiveness outside all the neighbouring churches before being publicly beaten with a rod!

THE ASH TREE OPERATIONS

Seventeenth-century Leicestershire was an equally lawless place. With no established police force, local constables were often unwilling to take action against criminals in remote areas.

Eaton in particular was a popular haunt for local criminals and murder, violence and looting was commonplace. So, to answer the problem, a group of ten local men became vigilantes. Establishing their hideout in the Eaton countryside, they became known as the 'Ash Tree Operatives' after the entrance to their hideout, which was through a hollowed-out ash tree.

NOTORIOUS CRIMES AND CRIMINALS

GEORGE DAVENPORT, HIGHWAYMAN

Born in 1758 in Wigston, George Davenport was Leicestershire's most famous highwayman.

George was apprenticed to a framework knitter, but he had no appetite for work, preferring to drink with his rowdy friends. George turned to crime for money when he left his apprenticeship, cutting his teeth on fraud. His favourite practice was to find an army recruitment sergeant, join up, and pocket the advance money paid to new recruits. After a session in the inn at the sergeant's expense, George would leave the unconscious recruiting officer and do a runner, often on a stolen horse. By his own account, George deserted from no fewer than forty regiments in this way.

George did eventually join up, serving as a British soldier during the American War of Independence, but after his army career folded, he returned home and took to the Leicestershire highways as a robber.

For eighteen years, he plied his trade and became mythologised as some sort of a Robin Hood figure who robbed the rich and gave to the poor of Oadby and Wigston.

One evening, he was drinking in the Bull's Head in Belgrave when he saw a poster offering a reward for his capture. 'I am George Davenport, catch me if you can,' he goaded his fellow drinkers, before hightailing it off the premises, leaving behind his dumbfounded would-be captors.

But in August 1797 George's luck ran out. A butcher he was attempting to rob bested him and handed him over to the constable. He was tried and convicted of highway robbery, and was hanged at Red Hill gallows. George, however, had the last laugh. It was customary for the hangman to claim everything belonging to an executed criminal 'outside the shroud'. George, wily to the end, went to his death with his shroud over his clothes – effectively cheating the hangman of his bounty.

George's son, William, joined the navy, serving as a sergeant in the Royal Marines. After leaving, he too ended up in the county gaol – but as head turnkey, rather than as a prisoner.

EARL FERRERS

Laurence Shirley, the 4th Earl Ferrers, owned estates in Leicestershire, Derbyshire and Northamptonshire but his main residence was at Staunton Harold Hall, near Ashby de la Zouch.

Ferrers was a womaniser and a drinker. He destroyed his marriage with his violent and erratic behaviour towards his wife, which was so bad she was granted a separation by Act of Parliament in 1758. As part of the separation, Ferrers was forced to make

a financial settlement on his wife, a fact he bitterly resented. It fell to his old family steward, John Johnson, to administer this allowance. Ferrers discovered Johnson was also secretly bestowing Lady Ferrers with extra income without his knowledge, which deepened his antipathy towards his servant.

On Sunday, 13 January 1760, Ferrers invited Johnson to visit the hall on the following Friday, the 18th, to discuss business. Ferrer's then sent away his live-in mistress and their children, plus the other servants, so that he and Johnson were alone.

At around 3 p.m., Ferrers and Johnson had a heated argument and Ferrers shot his steward. The wound was not fatal and Ferrers did call a Dr Kirkland to attend to Johnson, but while the medic was treating his patient, the earl continued to drunkenly abuse his victim before falling into a stupor. Before doing so, according to Kirkland he made the following admission:

> he told him that he had shot Johnson, but believed he was more frightened than hurt; that he had intended to shoot him dead, for that he was a villain, and deserved to die; 'but,' said he, 'now that I have spared his life, I desire you would do what you can for him.'

Johnson died the following day and Dr Kirkland enlisted the support of a number of local men to disarm and arrest the earl. The inquest brought in a verdict of wilful murder and so Ferrers was remanded in custody at Leicester Prison. As he was a peer of the realm, the Leicester Assizes did not have jurisdiction over him, so he was transferred to the Tower of London on 14 February and committed to the custody of Black Rod.

On 16 April 1760, in Westminster Hall, Ferrers pleaded insanity – which was not unfeasible as everyone who knew him already thought him mad. But after conducting his defence 'clearly and cogently' his fellow peers rejected his plea and, as the evidence left them no other choice, Ferrers was found guilty and sentenced to death. He was the last peer of the realm in Britain to suffer that fate.

Having been denied beheading – the usual mode of execution for a peer – on 5 May 1760 the earl found himself on his way to the death of a common criminal at Tyburn.

A special new gallows, complete with black baize, had been constructed for the occasion. The earl travelled in his own carriage, in his wedding suit, for 'he thought this at least as good an occasion for putting them on as that for which they were first made'. He died at around noon, having shown more style and courage at his death than on many occasions in life. His body was buried at St Pancras church after dissection, but twenty-two years later it was taken back to Staunton Harold and reinterred in the family crypt.

TOPSY TURVEY

John Massey of Bilstone was a farm labourer and famous local wrestler. He became known as Topsy Turvey for defeating his opponents by throwing them over his head.

Massey was also a known drunk with a violent temper. He was known to be cruel to his first wife, Sarah, who died in 1797. However, this did not deter a second woman from marrying him, despite the fact she had a young daughter. The union was not a happy one and its end was tragic. One evening in 1800, the family were out walking near Bilstone Mill. Massey and his wife had a violent argument that culminated in the wrestler losing his temper and brutally beating his wife before kicking her and her daughter into the millstream.

Mrs Massey died, but her daughter survived, leaving her as the prime witness. Massey was tried at Leicester Assizes and found guilty. He was sentenced to be hanged and his body gibbeted after his death. On 23 March 1801, he was executed at Red Hill in Birstall and a day later his body was transported for gibbeting in the parish where the crime was committed. The body was wrapped in chain and hanged from a metal ring on the gibbet post as a gruesome warning to passers-by. As late as 1818, the remains of Topsy Turvey reputedly remained in place.

JAMES COOK

In 1832, James Cook was a 21-year-old Leicester bookbinder with his own workshop on Wellington Street. But Cook was in trouble – money trouble.

Cook owed money to a London engraver called John Paas. On a fateful visit to Leicester, in May 1832, Paas visited Cook at his workshop to demand repayment. An argument ensued and Cook hit Paas on the head, killing him.

In a panic, Cook dismembered the body, and, drinking heavily to steady his nerve, began to try and dispose of the remains in his workshop fire. But Cook's fireplace was not built for such a grisly task. The fire was soon out of control and the neighbours alerted the authorities, who arrived to investigate.

An inebriated Cook explained he was disposing of a rotten piece of dog meat. But his visitors were not convinced and took the 'meat' away. On examination, it proved to be the pelvis and thigh of a human.

Paas's absence and the fact his pencil case was found at the scene helped identify him as the victim. Cook, in the meantime, attempted to flee to America – only to be apprehended as his boat was about to leave Liverpool docks.

He was found guilty at Leicester and sentenced to hang and be gibbeted – making him the last man in England whose remains suffered that fate.

PEPPERMINT BILLY

Born near Scalford, William 'Peppermint Billy' Brown gained his nickname from his father's occupation as a mint maker.

Billy did not follow in his father's footsteps. In 1843 he was sentenced to ten years' transportation for stealing a horse at Newtown Linford. He served his sentence in Tasmania and in 1856 returned to England.

But it was not long before Billy was again in trouble with the law. On 20 June 1856, the bodies of 70-year-old Thorpe Arnold tollgate keeper Edward Woodcock and his young grandson were found in the tollgate keeper's gatehouse. Mr Woodcock had been stabbed many times and shot. His grandson's throat was cut.

Billy was implicated because he had had an altercation with the elderly toll keeper two days earlier, when the old man refused him a drink of water. Perhaps more damning were certain items that could be associated with him found at the scene. A tobacco stopper and pistol of the type used by Australian bushrangers were found close to the bodies, and a bloodstained shirt was discovered dumped nearby.

A £20 reward was offered for Billy's capture and his description was circulated around the country. He was eventually arrested in Yorkshire and returned to Melton Mowbray to await trial.

Billy's protests of innocence came to nothing and he was convicted. His was the last public hanging in Leicestershire, on 25 July 1856, in front of a crowd of 25,000 who gathered outside

Welford Road prison. Billy made no speech but was calm and collected as he went to his death. His father, who witnessed his execution, certainly approved, as he was heard to say, 'Well done, Billy. Thas died a brick.'

A CONTROVERSIAL ACQUITTAL

On Saturday, 5 July 1919, the body of 21-year-old Annie Bella Wright was found lying next to her bicycle on Stretton Lane, Little Stretton. Initially it was thought that Bella had died in a freak fall. But careful examination of the scene by officer PC Hall revealed a .455 calibre bullet, trodden into the road surface near the body. Further investigation revealed Bella had been shot just below her left eye.

It seemed that a mysterious man on a green bicycle was key to events. He had been observed watching and following Bella on her fateful trip to Stretton. Eventually, a green bicycle was fished out of Leicester Canal. It was identified as belonging to Ronald Light, an ex-army officer and schoolteacher. Light had also been issued with a .455 revolver while in the army.

On his arrest, Light admitted he had dumped the bike for fear that it incriminated him. He also admitted to being with Bella on the day of her death but denied the killing.

Light was tried at Leicester Castle Assizes and was defended by one of the best advocates of the age, Sir Edward Marshall Hall. Despite the evidence, Light was acquitted, but many Leicester people believed he was guilty of the murder.

NOT SO NOTORIOUS CRIMES

THE MURDER OF THOMAS BARRETT

It was an ordinary August day in 1886 for the residents of Breedon on the Hill until James Banton, a local poacher, appeared running drunkenly down the High Street, waving a stick and announcing, 'I just killed a bobby!'

The 'bobby' was Thomas Barrett, one of a group of officers who had arrested Banton and a friend for poaching six months earlier. Banton and his associate had come across PC Barrett and decided to pick a fight with the policeman. But the fight ended with PC Barrett being beaten to death with his own baton.

Fortunately for him, Banton's friend had left the scene before the attack began, which led to his acquittal. But for Banton, his drunken altercation led to the noose.

PC WILLIAM WILKINSON

William Wilkinson was well liked in Sileby. A 'nice fellow who would rather see a man home than lock him up' was how locals remembered him. He was well thought of in the Leicestershire force too, earning himself a merit stripe for good conduct.

On 25 May 1903, just before leaving for his nightshift patrolling the streets of Sileby, PC Wilkinson's little girl cried, 'Daddy, I don't want you to go out again tonight.' PC Wilkinson reassured her that he would soon be home and left.

But he never came home, for not everyone thought well of PC Wilkinson. At around 11 p.m. Wilkinson investigated a rustling in the bushes around St Mary's churchyard. Suddenly, two figures sprang up from behind a gravestone, firing at Wilkinson, who reeled down the road for a few paces before falling down dead.

Local shoe hands Thomas Preston and Thomas Porter were arrested for the crime. They were known to bear a grudge against Wilkinson and his fellow officer PC Hall, who had arrested them previously for poaching and disorderly drinking. Preston once threatened to 'shoot the pair of you'.

On the day in question, both had been drinking heavily since midday and half an hour before the murder, Porter was heard to tell a friend, 'You may hear something in the morning.'

Officers went to Porter's house where the two were holed up. The pair, still clearly drunk and brandishing a shotgun, refused to surrender. A siege began that lasted until the next morning, by which time they had sobered sufficiently to see some sense and end their resistance. They were found guilty and were hanged at Leicester Prison, despite pleading their innocence until the end.

A QUESTION OF TIME

William Palmer was an itinerant fish seller. In January 1911, he made the journey to Lutterworth from Folkstone to sell his wares.

The day after he left the district for home, a local widow, Mrs Ann Harris, was found strangled in her home. Scattered around her were her savings. Questions were asked and Palmer fell under suspicion because he paid for his train fare home with a handful of silver coins – when the day before he had been penniless.

On 28 January 1911, Palmer was arrested for Mrs Harris's murder. He denied the charges, claiming he had found the money, and although there was no other evidence against him, he was held in custody for five months on various pretexts.

At the end of this period, the landlord of the Rugby Hotel where Palmer broke his journey home decided to clean out the toilet cisterns – and found a watch, gold chain and purse identified as belonging to Mrs Harris.

Palmer was tried at Leicester Assizes for murder. One expert witness claimed the watch had only been in the cistern for a few days, while another believed it had been there for a couple of months. Either way, this meant that it could not have been placed there by Palmer. But when pressed, the second expert agreed the few months could actually have been five. This was sufficient to convict him.

'I am as innocent as a newborn babe,' Palmer declared as sentence was passed.

Palmer may well have been innocent of Mrs Palmer's murder. But he had served time for murder in South Africa as a teenager and was wanted for a murder in Manchester. He fought all the way to the gallows on the day of his execution, yelling at officials, 'Are you going to let these fellows murder me?'

THE AMOROUS HIGHWAYMAN

Jack Ovet was born in Nottingham and was a shoemaker by trade. But like so many who took to a life of crime in the eighteenth century, he wanted more from life. Jack liked to drink and aspired to be a gentleman, so he took to the road as a highwayman.

Ovet did reasonably well from his new career and developed a reputation for a certain gallantry. On one occasion, one of his victims claimed Ovet had only bested him because he took him by surprise. Ovet graciously returned the £20 he had taken from the man and challenged him to make good his claim in a one-to-one fight with swords. Ovet won – and reclaimed the stolen £20.

But events took a more romantic turn when Ovet robbed the Worcester stagecoach. Several young women handed over their valuables to the highwaymen that day. But one of them stole his heart. As he robbed her, Ovet reputedly said:

> Madam, cast not your eyes down, neither cover your face with those modest blushes; your charms have softened my temper, and I am no more the man I was. What I have taken from you (through mere necessity at present) is only borrowed; for as no object on earth ever had such an effect on me as you, assure yourself that if you please to tell me where I may direct to you, I'll upon honour make good your loss to the very utmost.

Somewhat surprisingly, the lady gave the highwayman her address and in a week she received a letter from him – not to return her money but to propose!

> Madam,
> These few lines are to acquaint you that though I lately had the cruelty to rob you of twenty guineas, yet you committed a greater robbery at the same time in robbing me of my heart; on which you may behold yourself enthroned, and all my faculties paying their homage to your unparalleled beauty. Therefore, be pleased to propose but the method how I may win your belief ... For by all my hopes, by all those rites that crown a happy union, by the rosy tincture of your checks, and by your all-subduing eyes, I prize you above all the world ... Let us taste the pleasures which Cupid commands, and for that unmerited favour I shall become another man, to make you happy. So requesting the small boon of a favourable answer to be sent me to Mr Walker's, who keeps an ale-house at the sign of the Bell in Thornbury, in Gloucestershire, give me leave to subscribe myself your most humble servant to command for ever.

The lady, however, was not seduced – and more than a little annoyed her money had not been returned. She replied:

> You have already broken your word in not sending what you villainously took from me, but not valuing that, let me tell you, for fear you should have too great a conceit of yourself, that you are the first, to my remembrance, whom I ever hated; and sealing my hatred with the hopes of quickly reading your dying speech, in case you die in London, I presume to subscribe myself yours never to command.

Finding himself unlucky in love, the rest of Ovet's luck quickly followed. After a botched robbery in Leicestershire, he was pursued, caught and condemned to hang on 5 May 1708. But for his amorous interlude, his career would have been totally unremarkable.

MURDEROUS MINERS

In 1877 three Coalville miners were found guilty of murdering a peddler. On the scaffold, one of them confessed that the other two were innocent and he alone was responsible for the crime: the authorities still hanged all three.

MOTORING OFFENCES

With the advent of the twentieth century, motoring offences began to become a category of crime in themselves. The year 1899 saw the first speeding prosecution in Leicestershire when a motorist was caught in Glenfield. He was fined 15 shillings for travelling just in excess of 18mph!

That was only the beginning. From 1923, Leicester City Police used an unmarked motorbike – a Triumph SD – to catch speeding motorists. The model had just come second in the Isle of Man TT and held a number of speed records at the time. It was chosen by PC Thomas William Haywood, who was assigned the bike. Dressed like a gamekeeper, the young PC patrolled the roads and reported two

drivers on his first day and four on his second. Their penalty was a
40-shilling fine and the loss of their driver's licence for six months.

HANNAH READ

When Hannah Read's husband deserted her and their five children
to flee from his creditors, it was perhaps understandable that she
took up with a man called Waterfield and had his child. James Read
was gone for two years, but when he returned home in 1825, he
demanded Hannah return to him at the marital home in Foxton.

Hannah agreed, but on the day of her return she suddenly sent for
her brother-in-law. She told him that on the journey home, James
had 'run away from her mad and had jumped into the water [at
Foxton Lock] and drowned himself'.

Hannah's brother-in-law did not believe her and the next day she
was arrested. Her husband's body was recovered from the lock and
witnesses came forward telling a very different story to Hannah.
At her trial, they claimed that Hannah had threatened to 'do for'
James. After only fifteen minutes of deliberation, the jury found her
guilty of James's murder.

Hannah's pleas for clemency as a mother failed and with death
finally inevitable, she confessed. She said she distracted James by
asking him for some money and as he reached into his pocket, she
had pushed him into the canal.

On the morning of her execution, 5 August 1825, Hannah was
taken to the county bridewell. Here, she was attached to a sledge
rather than loaded into a cart. This was an additional punishment
because her crime was counted as petty treason because she had
murdered her husband. In front of quite a considerable crowd she
was dragged to her execution and after attending the chaplain, taken
to the scaffold and hanged.

Hannah Read's case was publicised in twenty papers around the
country, to act as a warning to other wives who might wish to be
rid of their husbands – no matter what the justification.

COMIC CRIMES

THE DRUNKEN NUN OF QUORN

In December 1885, a Sister Mary Frances of the 'convent Quorndon' was taken before Loughborough Petty Sessions and charged with assaulting local manufacturer's wife, Mrs W. Wright. Sister Mary had visited the Wright house on 16 December to ask for contributions to the relief of the local homeless. Mrs Wright declined – probably because the nun seemed somewhat the worse for wear! Sister Mary then asked for a donation of brandy for a poor woman one of the sisters was nursing. Mrs Wright – perhaps to get rid of her – said she'd send the brandy if Sister Mary would give her the address. Realising she was getting nowhere, the inebriated nun began to beat Mrs Wright between the shoulders until the lady's servants pushed her out the door. However, the stroppy Sister then forced her way in a second time and when she was again evicted, began to shake the doors and windows.

Once she had sobered up, the repentant nun wrote to Mrs Wright apologising for 'anything that had occurred'. Despite having no memory of events, she denied the assault but was found guilty and was ordered to pay 15 shillings or face seven days in prison.

ROAD RAGE IN QUORN

Road rage is sadly not a modern phenomenon. In 1896, William Richardson, a Quorn butcher was accused of trying to run Charles Hodgkin off his bike after Hodgkin had the temerity to ring his bell and overtake Richardson's vehicle. In response, Richardson sped up and despite Mr Hodgkin slowing to allow him to pass, the butcher proceeded to zig-zag across the road to prevent the cycle from passing. Richardson was travelling so fast he nearly collided with an oncoming vehicle. This had the effect of stopping him and allowed Mr Hodgkin to pass him again.

But Richardson sped after him and at Mountsorrel caught up, calling to him 'Stop! I will stop you!' Richardson then overtook him, but Mr Hodgkin later found him in the road at Mountsorrel Hill, after finally colliding with another vehicle.

Once summoned, Richardson blamed the cyclist for his speeding. But Richardson was the worse for drink according to the policeman at the scene and the bench agreed, convicting Richardson of drink driving and attempting to run a cyclist down. He was fined £2.

And the vehicle in which this reckless pursuit occurred? A horse and cart!

6

GHOSTLY GOINGS-ON

HAUNTED HOUSES

BELGRAVE HALL

Belgrave Hall was once a grand country house. Now Belgrave is a suburb of Leicester and the house a museum.

But it seems some of the house's former residents have not moved on. Odd smells of baking bread and gingerbread waft through the rooms when no one is cooking, and hushed voices and mysterious footsteps have been heard about its corridors.

The hall's famous Grey or Green Lady is believed to be Charlotte Ellis, one of seven sisters who lived at the hall in the nineteenth century. Charlotte died there aged 81 in 1917, still a spinster. Her spirit reputedly roams the gardens. It was here on 23 December 1998 that CCTV apparently spotted her ghost when a misty white shape was captured on film. But this theory was debunked by a series of paranormal investigators, who claimed it was instead a leaf falling in front of the camera.

The Grey Lady may not be alone at Belgrave Hall. Paranormal experts believe she shares the hall with a 'negative male energy' upstairs, as well as a child who died of tuberculosis and the ghost of a man who was killed in a fall.

PAPILLON HALL

Papillon Hall used to be a mile west of Lubenham near Lutterworth before it was demolished in the 1950s. But the legend of its ghost – and maybe the restless spirit itself – still remains.

The hall was built in 1622 by the Papillon family on the site of a holy well once belonging to Leicester Abbey. But its sinister reputation dates back to the time of the great-grandson of the original builder: David Papillon, or 'Pamps'.

Pamps was a handsome man with a sinister reputation. He was believed to have harmful hypnotic powers. He also reputedly kept a Spanish mistress imprisoned in the attic of the house.

This mistress is said to have died in 1715 although her burial was never recorded. Soon afterwards, Pamps married and left Papillon Hall and the area. But he left behind a portrait of himself and a pair of lady's dancing shoes, with strict instructions that neither should be removed from the hall.

All was well at the hall as long as the objects remained in place – as future occupants discovered to their cost. When the Bosworth family sold the hall, they bequeathed its contents to one of their daughters. The new owner, Lord Hopeton, and his household were quickly plagued by unexplained knockings and misfortunes. Events culminated one terrifying night in 1866 when the entire household gathered in the lobby while they listened to the sounds of furniture being thrown violently around the empty drawing room. On investigation everything remained in its rightful place.

The shoes and portrait were traced and reinstated. But history repeated itself when the shoes were loaned to the Paris Exhibition of 1900. The family in residence at the time had to move out for the duration of the shoes' absence.

The shoes were then secured in the hall in a wall safe. But during alterations to the hall in 1903 they were removed again. A worker was subsequently killed by a falling brick, while the owner, Captain Bellville, was hurt in a pony and trap accident.

During the Second World War, the hall was requisitioned by the government to house American servicemen. A group of the soldiers decided to test out the curse. They soon came to regret their decision and quickly returned the shoes to the hall.

So, who was the ghost – Pamps or his dead mistress? Pamps' portrait seems to have had an unsettling reputation, with many owners finding it evil. But the shoes seem to be the key, so perhaps it is the mysterious Spanish mistress who is the restless spirit. During the 1903 renovations, the skeleton of a woman was found bricked up behind a wall. Could this explain why there is no record of her burial?

On the hall's demolition, the shoes were reclaimed by a Papillon descendant and now lie in Market Harborough Museum. Meanwhile, the grounds of Papillon Hall became a farm. But it seems that even though the house has gone, a presence remains. The Hughes family who own the farm have heard strange noises around the old stable blocks, which still survive, as well as the eerie feeling of a presence wandering about the land.

WIGSTON COLLEGE

Wigston College stands on the site of what was once one of the grandest houses in the area, Heatherley House. But although the house is gone, it seems its last owner remains.

In the 1980s, a cleaner at the college reported hearing a woman calling her name – despite being alone. The caretakers explained that it was the former owner of the old house, who caused no harm but did like to tap people on the shoulder and otherwise disrupt them. Sometime later, the cleaner saw the ghost for the first time, crossing a path by the workshops and walking through a wall, dressed in a long black dress with a bunch of keys at her waist.

The ghost is reputedly the second wife of the house's original owner. After her husband's death, the county council offered to buy the house and grounds to build a college, but the lady refused and threatened to curse any establishment built on her land. But when the old lady was finally taken into care, the guardians of the estate sold the house and grounds.

Heatherley House was subsequently demolished and Wigston College constructed. But at her death, its former owner seems to have returned to watch over her old home. Reputedly a good old lady in life, she continues to be so in death as none of her manifestations have been sinister.

OTHER HAUNTED HOUSES

Not all of Leicestershire's haunted houses are grand ones. The residents of a terraced housing association property on School Lane in Loughborough never felt comfortable in their home. Soon after moving in, lights and the microwave began to inexplicably switch themselves on and off, and posters rearranged themselves on the walls.

The tenant contacted a medium, who told her a ghost called Nigel was haunting the property. Nigel had been a man in his thirties with a low mental age whose parents hid him away. But when ghostbuster Don Philips offered to investigate, he identified a further forty-nine spirits at the property. Among these were a 6-year-old boy killed in a fire and a man who hanged himself in the cellar. Don managed to help most of the ghosts to find peace. However, some remained.

In 1778, a house in Earl Shilton was said to be plagued by its former long-dead occupant. Tables and chairs danced about the room, while pewter dishes jumped off the shelves. The alarm caused by the poltergeist grew when wigs and hats flew off the heads of their wearers. Villagers agreed that the disturbed spirit was a local man who could not rest in his grave because he had been defrauded in life.

Once a grand house owned by the Winstanley family, Braunstone Hall in Leicester is reputedly haunted by May Winstanley, who died as a novice nun. It seems May returned to her family home after her untimely death, as her ghost was seen by servants, members of the Winstanley family, and by staff when the house became a school.

Now a conference centre, Bosworth Hall in Market Bosworth once had a perpetual wet bloodstain and is haunted by a Grey Lady, reputedly Ann Dixie, who bled to death in the eighteenth century after being caught in a mantrap set by her father to capture her gardener lover.

Bushby Old Hall, demolished in 1965, only yielded its ghosts as its walls came down. As demolition proceeded, perfectly sturdy parts of the building began falling down of their own accord, workers heard strange noises and events culminated in one terrified builder running away after an encounter with a spectral old lady. The ghost was identified as Mary, a former maid at the hall who took her own life. The disturbances – and the ghost – disappeared with the last of the rubble.

In 1906 at The Spring's House, Lutterworth, a maid woke suddenly to see a young man in old-fashioned clothing standing at the foot of her bed. He then vanished into thin air, so terrifying the girl that she refused to stay overnight in the house again. The phantom was believed to be John Cook, a resident of the house fifty years earlier who was murdered on the premises.

The first person to report a ghost at The Cedars in Kegworth was the Irish poet Thomas Moore, who wrote to a friend complaining of it in 1812. The phantom is supposedly that of a murdered butler, and at one time the bloodstain of the crime was impossible to wash away.

HAUNTED PUBS

THE TALBOT INN

The Talbot Inn lies 3 miles from Leicester city centre. It was originally built in the 1600s and was the last stop for condemned felons on the way to the Red Hill gallows at Birstall. Many of the condemned also returned to the inn after their visit to the gallows, as one of the inn's outbuildings was used to accommodate the medical dissections of the remains of those not claimed for burial.

Unsurprisingly, several mysterious figures have been seen drifting around the inn's gardens, believed to be the restless spirits of those unfortunate souls. But the inn is also haunted on the inside. Pool balls frequently knock together of their own accord, while drinkers experience the classic chilly spots. Here, the ghosts include a cheerful young boy and a young woman brushing her dishevelled hair – believed to be the ghost of a woman who died in childbirth.

THE BLUE BOAR INN

Sadly demolished in the nineteenth century, Leicester's Blue Boar Inn was reputedly haunted by the ghost of one of its landladies, Agnes Clarke, who was murdered for her money in 1613. After the inn was demolished, a new pub of the same name was established on Southgate Street. Agnes's ghost duly followed.

Frederick Mason, a landlord of the inn in 1958, refused to believe in the ghost despite warnings from his regulars. When he fell down the cellar stairs and broke his ankle, he put it down to an unlucky accident. Even cracking a rib in a coughing fit brought on by a bad cold was put down to bad luck. But all disbelief was suspended when he woke one night to see a white figure moving towards his bed. Agnes's ghost, now satisfied that Mr Mason was now a believer, never visited him again.

OTHER GHOSTLY PUBS

Agnes Clarke is not the only publican unable to call time on her duties. The spirit of Alice Johnson, once landlady of The Royal Oak at Great Dalby, also can't let go of her former occupation. Her fiery spirit pokes people at the bar who annoy her and throws books off bookshelves. Likewise, John Fothergill, landlord of The Three Swans Hotel in Market Harborough, reputedly haunts the portrait of him on the premises, causing disturbances if it is removed.

The Anne of Cleves in Melton Mowbray dates back to 1384. This ancient building on Burton Street was once a monk's chantry house. Its present-day patrons number the dead as well as the living, including a White Lady in the garden and a gentleman sitting on a bench near the back door. Ghost hunters have identified one of the spirits as Alfred Syetys, a local axe murderer.

The Union Inn in Hinckley is reputedly haunted by a 'regular' who sits at his favourite table reading, as well as a mischievous child and several soldiers. Its cellar is haunted by a gentleman highwayman who may well have met his end in the town square and was one of the bodies of the executed regularly stored in the cellar.

The White Hart in Ashby de la Zouch was once used to detain prisoners due to be executed at the nearby castle. The pub was investigated by Spirit Team UK, who detected phantom children and an elderly lady. Mysterious mist also manifests around the beer barrels and a spirit of indeterminate sex is often glimpsed. Its head hangs to one side, suggesting that they were hanged.

In the 1970s, it was reported that the cellar of The Old Plough in Birstall was haunted by a phantom barrel mover.

Renovations to The White Horse in Broughton Astley in 2011 set off a series of unearthly events. Soon after the old cellar floor was dug up, radios began to turn themselves on (even if they were unplugged), objects moved of their own accord or were thrown by unseen hands, and the attic doors opened. Black shadows were spotted in mirrors and the figure of a woman was seen about the otherwise empty pub.

Not all ghosts are sinister. The Woodman's Stroke in Rothley has a resident spirit called Gregory. A friendly spook, Gregory is supposed to guarantee good luck to anyone who spots him.

The male ghost as The Belper Arms in Newton Burgoland is notorious for slapping or stroking female waitresses – and trying to smother male waiters! The apparition only manifests at set times of the day – either 3.55 a.m. or 15.55 p.m. – earning himself the name 'Five to four Fred'.

HAUNTED HOLY PLACES

GRACE DIEU PRIORY

In the thirteenth century, Roesia de Verdun, an independent, wealthy landowner, built Grace Dieu Priory for the Augustinian order of nuns. Roesia was determined to avoid remarriage – so

she became Grace Dieu's first prioress. The
priory became the site of a hospital for
local poor people until the Dissolution
of the Monasteries.

Today, the priory lies in ruins, as does
the Tudor house built on the site after
the Dissolution. But it is not deserted.
Various grey and white misty shapes have
been sighted on and around the ruins. These
figures include a White Lady, who has been seen
walking from the priory to the nearby bus stop.
Several local bus drivers have been unnerved when
they have stopped for a woman in white – only to have her
disappear as soon as the bus doors open to admit her!

Other encounters have been more sinister, with a council
workman on the site refusing to work there again after he was
pushed over by an invisible force.

Theories abound about the identity of the ghosts. Some state
one is Agnes Litherland, a sixteenth-century abbess walled up in
the priory after she gave birth to a child. But it could equally be the
restless Roesia de Verdun, who is said to roam the grounds as a
result of her grave being disturbed in the nineteenth century.

SWITHLAND RECTORY

Demolished after the First World War, Swithland Rectory was said
to be haunted by the daughter of its nineteenth-century rector.
On returning home to prepare the house for the family, she was
murdered by their drunken butler, who then slit his own throat in
remorse once he had sobered up.

Awful screams were said to come from the rectory at night, as
well as sightings of the ghostly butler, hacking at his throat.

After the demolition of the house, local legend tells that the
figure of a lady in a grey dress, carrying a slab of stone from the
rectory, was seen heading to the church. The Grey Lady is now seen
infrequently haunting the churchyard, mainly appearing around
weddings, christenings and funerals.

OTHER HAUNTED HOLY PLACES

St Margaret's church, Leicester. A bell-ringing poltergeist and an old lady relocated to the church after their original haunt in the vicarage was demolished in the 1960s.

Church of St Edward King and Martyr, Castle Donington. In 1950, a brother and sister were visiting St Edward's when they got into a conversation with a vicar they did not know. The man explained his name was Father Dougal and that he had been based at the church before leaving. It was only later that the couple discovered that Father Dougal had indeed been vicar of the church – until his death in 1906.

While exploring the grounds of Mount St Bernard Abbey in Coalville in the 1990s, a woman visitor suddenly noticed a man behind her. He was quite unremarkable, with ginger hair and a tan leather jacket. However, as he passed the lady, he melted away into the shrubbery ahead. The mysterious man isn't the only ghost spotted at the abbey. In 1935, a local groom spotted the ghostly apparition of a monk near a wall by the abbey's pump house. It turned out that one of the monks had died suddenly in the building just hours before the appearance of the apparition.

PUBLIC BUILDINGS

THE GUILDHALL, LEICESTER

Leicester's Guildhall has had a varied life. Since its construction in the fourteenth century, it has been the meeting house for the town guilds, the council house, police headquarters and prison. Today it is a museum. So it's no wonder it's credited with its fair share of ghosts – both human and animal. Locked doors in the Mayor's Parlour have been known to spring open of their own accord. A phantom cat and dog haunt the courtyard and Great Hall respectively, and a tormented cavalier and the spirit of a policeman also roam the grounds.

A White Lady with a fondness for Deuteronomy 18:10 reputedly haunts the library. Curators regularly find the pages of the displayed Bible turned to this passage, which relates to witchcraft and divination.

THE HARBOROUGH THEATRE, MARKET HARBOROUGH

Once the site of The Green Dragon Inn, this theatre has the reputation of being haunted by the spirit of an elderly sea captain who retired to the inn in his old age. Quite what an old sea dog was doing inland is unknown, but his spirit is attached to his old residence and manifests as cold spots, a disembodied voice and footsteps.

But the ghost could also be a former maid of the coaching inn called Hannah. This notorious flirt was supposedly murdered by her lover in a fit of rage. After a violent argument, the couple disappeared. Her lover was never seen again but Hannah's body was later discovered in the River Welland, 10 miles from the town.

LOUGHBOROUGH'S OLD MAGISTRATES' COURT

Loughborough's old court also has its ghosts. Built in 1860 as a police station, it has sat empty since 2008, but footsteps and whispers have been heard about its abandoned rooms and corridors.

But the ghosts were active long before the building's abandonment. In the 1960s, a man spending the night in the cells struck up a conversation with the prisoner next door. When he was released the next day, he asked to say goodbye to his neighbour – only to be told the cell had been empty all night.

CASUALTIES OF WAR

Leicestershire has seen its fair share of battles and bloodshed throughout time. So it's no surprise that it also has its fair share of military ghostly goings-on.

GHOSTLY INVADERS

Wigston Harcourt housing estate is partly built on a field called Heards Close. In the 1980s, before the houses were built, a woman and her son spent an uncomfortable couple of nights camped on the site. On the first night, cries and moans were heard, as well as the clash of swords. The following evening the woman was woken by what she initially thought was her son telling her to 'get up'. But on waking, she was greeted not by her child but by another, pale as a corpse and dressed in white.

Once the houses were built, residents saw a number of hazy figures marching in armour, before fading away at a nearby graveyard. In the 1880s, gravediggers had found fragments of broken shields, armour and swords, attributed to Danish invaders who pillaged Wigston in AD 876. Could it be that Heards Close is haunted by this ghostly battle?

BOSWORTH FIELD, SUTTON CHENEY

Bosworth Field is arguably the county's most famous battlefield. The site of the Battle of Bosworth in 1485, it has a reputation for being haunted. Andrew James Wright in his book *Ghosts and Hauntings in and Around Leicestershire* cites a story from the 1980s when a group of visitors attended a steam rally on the site. One lady visitor began to feel most unusual. Despite the bright sunshine, she felt the day was cold and grey and began to talk to her companions about 'the hill'. Becoming very distressed, the lady asked for a horse. She could hear shouting and screaming and the sounds of battle.

The hill she identified was Ambion Hill, where the battle reputedly took place. Even more eerily, her experience occurred on 22 August – the anniversary of the Battle of Bosworth.

EERIE AIRMEN

The former British Shoe Corporation warehouse at Scudamore Road, Braunstone Frith, boasts the ghost of a Second World War RAF airman, seen fleeing in panic. The smell of burning often accompanies the spirit, mysteriously dissipating when he disappears. The apparition is supposedly that of the pilot of a plane that crashed at the site in 1942, when it was a wartime training facility.

Bottesford also boasts a similar haunting at its old RAF base, which closed at the end of the Second World War. Weird lights and the drone of plane engines have been heard and a solitary figure in a sheepskin jacket and flying helmet has been sighted near the control tower.

GHOSTS OF ROAD AND RAIL

LEY LINES

Frog Island in Leicester was once part of the town's Abbey Meadows before it became an island in the late eighteenth century after being annexed by the completion of the Soar Navigation.

The island quickly became a prime location for textile mills in the nineteenth century. But it was not until the late 1960s and early '70s that the Britella hosiery factory on New Pingle Street manifested its ghost, a disruptive spirit that caused much industrial unrest. An evil presence was felt in the factory, with several people being prodded by unseen fingers and a black mist manifesting on the premises. The workers threatened to strike because of the paranormal troublemaker so a mild exorcism was carried out and the activity calmed down.

There is no clue as to the identity of the spirit, but the location of the factory suggests a possible cause. 'Pingle' refers to an old track. This could refer to the old ley line that reputedly runs through the street – with the Britella factory at its furthest end. Could it be that the Britella ghost was no ghost at all but rather the power of the Pingle Street ley line?

A TOPSY-TURVY GHOST

In the mid-1990s, a motorist driving along Gibbet Lane in Bilstone hit a large grey-haired man in a trench coat. The driver stopped the car and checked for the injured man, but he was nowhere to be seen.

The shocked driver called the police and a search ensued. But the mystery man was not to be found.

Others have seen a similar ghost. Is he John Massey, known as Topsy Turvey, whose body was displayed in the lane's eponymous gibbet? Massey was a violent drunk who drowned his wife and nearly killed her young daughter in the early nineteenth century. He was hanged at Red Hill in Birstall, but his body was returned to the parish the murder was committed in and displayed in a gibbet.

But if Massey does not haunt the area, it is possible his victims do. In 1979 a motorist saw two figures staring at the gibbet post – the dripping wet figures of a woman and young girl.

GHOSTLY TRAIN SPOTTING

The old line near Thorpe Satchville was the spot where a dog walker spotted the ghostly vision of an early railway outing. The woman briefly glimpsed the vision of a train with a tall smokestack and three carriages, surrounded by men in top hats and ladies in crinolines, chatting happily, before they faded away.

MARY QUINN

Harry Gamble was a bus conductor on the number 616 that ran from St Margaret's bus station in Leicester to Uppingham, a small town in Rutland. Harry noticed that a pretty young lady who got off at the village of Tugby was becoming a regular passenger. She told Harry her name was Mary Quinn and that she lived with her parents in a cottage with a blue door with a leaded window that was surrounded by roses.

One day it rained hard. Mary was only wearing a light summer dress, so Harry lent her his raincoat so she could return home dry. He never saw her again.

Disturbed by her sudden disappearance, Harry went to Tugby on his day off to see if he could find her. He located her house by its description. But when he mentioned Mary's name to the lady who opened the door, she slammed it in his face, much distressed.

A puzzled Harry called out to a neighbour to find out what he had done wrong. The man led Harry to the local graveyard and showed him a gravestone – dedicated to Mary Quinn. The date of death was two years earlier. What was more, draped over the back of the stone was Harry's coat.

OTHER GHOSTS OF ROAD AND RAIL

Rothley railway station is reputedly haunted by its former stationmaster and a ghostly dog and its owner – both killed on the line just before the start of the Second World War. A phantom woman in blue also haunts the station waiting room.

In 1967 and 1994, witnesses at Belvoir Castle Rally Track, Knipton, saw a mounted figure on horseback, dressed in a long grey coat and believed to be a highwayman.

In 2009, a startled driver on the M1 at Castle Donington spotted a man dressed in a green jacket, dark trousers and with something on his head standing in the middle lane of the motorway, just past junction 24. When she glanced back in her rear-view mirror, to check if the man was OK, the driver found the man had completely disappeared.

Platform One of Loughborough Central Station is said to be haunted by a transparent railway worker, dressed in an old-fashioned uniform, holding an oil lamp.

ALLOTMENTS AND GARDENS

The former site of the allotments on Newton Lane, Wigston, used to be haunted by an old gardener. Neglectful allotmenteers would often feel his wrath. One was badly stung by wasps that appeared in a nest in his shed. Another's water butt reputedly dried up overnight, while a further unfortunate stuck a fork in his foot – all apparently at the behest of the otherwise benign ghost who manifested as a pipe-smoking old man, dressed in baggy trousers, tied at the knee with string, a baggy coat and cloth cap.

FAMOUS GHOSTS

The ruins of Lady Jane Grey's former home in Bradgate Park are reputedly visited by the doomed queen's spirit every Christmas when she makes the journey from the old church to the ruins of the house in a carriage.

John of Gaunt is said to haunt Leicester Castle, reputedly the favourite of his many residences.

Even before archaeologists discovered his grave on the site of Greyfriars' friary in Leicester, the ghost of Richard III was said to roam the streets of the neighbourhood. But the dead king's spirit may also have turned up elsewhere in Leicestershire: at Donington le Heath manor house where Richard reputedly spent the night before the fateful Battle of Bosworth.

Amateur paranormal researchers apparently recorded the king's voice in 2013. A spirit was contacted in the room and when asked 'What is your name?' it replied 'Richard.'

GHOSTLY MISCELLANEA

THE BLEEDING GRAVESTONE

The spirit of Richard Smith, a young saddler killed by a recruiting sergeant in 1727, was said to haunt a tree in Hinckley.

Smith was watching the sergeant on Duck Puddle Lane as he attempted to lure new recruits for the army. He kept calling out and correcting the sergeant – pointing out, for instance, that the local pub was not named 'The George' after the king but instead after the saint. As the saddler showed up more of the sergeant's ignorance, the crowd began to jeer and the soldier lost his temper. He turned upon the young saddler and ran him through with his halberd, pinning him to a nearby oak tree.

Every April the saddler's friends visited his grave – and reputedly blood-red moisture would ooze from the headstone.

THE LOST WIFE OF BLABY

One April night in 1995, at around 8.30 p.m., two people driving to a party stopped for a smoke in their car. While taking their break, they saw the outline of a woman in a long coat walking near a steep bank.

Turning on the car lights to check the woman was all right, they found the figure was nowhere to be seen. Thinking nothing more of it, they finished their cigarettes and carried on to the party.

Towards the end of the evening, people began to tell ghost stories. One of them included the tale of a phantom woman who was said to search for the ghost of her husband who drowned in 1923 at Blaby Ford – the very spot the partygoers had stopped for their smoke.

ABBEY PUMPING STATION MUSEUM

The former pumping station near the National Space Centre is reputedly haunted by the ghost of a worker who fell to his death in the beam engine house. The ethereal engineer makes his presence felt by playing with the lights and making noises in the basement.

THE MILLER OF KIBWORTH

A local miller of Kibworth entered into a drinking contest at a local pub. Fearful that the miller would win, his companions laced his drinks with gin – rendering the miller deeply unconscious. When the miller could not be roused and gave no signs of life, he was duly declared dead – and so buried. But soon after his internment, noises were heard from his grave that suggested the unfortunate miller had, in fact, been sleeping off his very heavy session
– only to awake in the most horrible and lethal of circumstances. The tragic miller's spirit has often been seen wandering about the graveyard.

7

FOOD AND DRINK

'Shake a Leicestershire man by the collar and you may hear the beans rattle in his belly' (Magna Britannia, 1820)

FRUIT AND VEG

'BEAN BELLY LEICESTERSHIRE'

Leicestershire was once known for its prolific cultivation of beans – particularly the broad bean, which was the staple of many a country diet. So prolific was the bean in the Leicestershire diet that the county was known as 'Bean Belly Leicestershire'.

The popularity of beans as a staple crop and favourite food led to some of the major places of cultivation being named after them – such as the village of Barton in the Beans, near Hinckley and Bosworth.

FRUITS: OLD AND NEW

The rich clay soils of Leicestershire make them the perfect place to grow apples and there are plenty of local varieties. Barnack Orange, Croft Sharp and Belvoir Seedling are local varieties for desserts and cider making, as is the Annie Elizabeth Cooking Apple. The Packington apple was believed lost until 2015, when the Leicestershire Heritage Apple Project finally discovered a tree in the village of Tonge.

The Annie Elizabeth is a sweet apple with a sad story behind its name. Samuel Greatorex, a magistrate's clerk of Leicester, developed the apple in 1857. But the fruit had to wait for its name until 1866 – when Greatorex named it after his deceased baby daughter.

The Syston White Plum is a well-known county
variety, grown since the late 1800s. Oval, with
a thin yellow skin, it is harvested in September
and famed as a dessert plum and the
symbol of Syston.

Oadby and Wigston hosted a yearly
Apple Day every October from 2008 to 2015,
promoting Leicestershire's apple varieties. Held at
Brocks Hill Country Park, where a community orchard
was planted in 2001, the event celebrated all things apple:
from juice to honey and cider – and the Leicestershire
Heritage Apple Project.

Naturally tomatoes are not a native fruit of Leicestershire, but the
county has its own heritage tomato. The former George Nursery
at Blaby grew the Blaby Special from 1912. It was much favoured
by local people for its bright red colour and juicy flesh. During
the Second World War it was especially popular and locals would
queue for up to half a mile for their chance to acquire the tomato
treat. But the farm went out of business after the war and the
Blaby Special was lost. That was until the seeds were rediscovered
in a seed bank in the Netherlands.

In 2006 the people of Blaby were reunited with their tomato
and they have been growing it on their allotments ever since. To
celebrate the return of their favourite fruit, since August 2010 Blaby
has held its own annual tomato festival.

FAMOUS FOODS AND LOCAL RECIPES

CHEESE

Stilton is probably the most famous cheese of the county, known as
'The King of English Cheeses' because of its full-bodied fragrance
and delicate veins of blue mould.

There are various origin stories about Stilton. One attributes its
creation to a Mrs Pawlet, a cheesemaker from Wymondham near

Melton Mowbray, who in 1730 made a cream cheese, which she sent to a relative, Cooper Thornhill, the landlord of The Bell Inn in Stilton, Huntingdon.

The cheese became popular with the inn's customers and was soon known as Stilton Cheese after the village that sold it. The Bell Inn was situated along the main London to Edinburgh road – ensuring that Stilton's reputation soon spread the length of the country.

Another story credits Quenby Hall as the birthplace of Stilton, where it was reputedly known as Lady Beaumont's cheese. Yet another claims the cheese was the original creation of a Mrs Orton of Little Dalby.

Historical research confirms some elements of the legends – but also proves that Stilton evolved over time, rather than being the product of any one individual or place. Stilton was indeed named after the place it was originally distributed from. However, a Stilton-like cheese was being produced in Leicestershire long before 1730. It may even date back to the fourteenth century.

Richard Bradley published a recipe for a hard cream cheese, pressed and boiled in its whey like Stilton, in a newsletter in 1723. Daniel Defoe, in his *Tours Through the Villages of England and Wales,* also knew of the cheese, referring to it in 1724 as 'The English Parmesan'.

It seems that Thornhill actually commissioned Mrs Pawlet to make the cheese for him in 1743 – after he had already established a trade for a local cream cheese. Mrs Pawlet subsequently recruited other cheesemakers to work with her, using her recipe for a blue-veined cheese – the same recipe we know today.

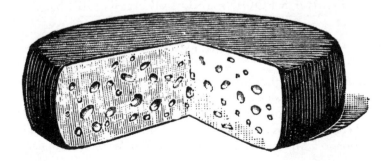

Until the nineteenth century, all Stilton was produced within 20 miles of Melton Mowbray. Today, true Stilton is only produced in six dairies, one being Websters Dairy in Saxelbye. In 1996, it was one of the few cheeses granted a Protected Designation of Origin by the European Commission.

Red Leicester is a millstone-shaped farmhouse cheese originally known as the Leicestershire cheese until the 'red' – caused originally by the addition of extract of carrots to distinguish it from other local cheeses – was added to the name in the seventeenth century.

Red Leicester reached London via Leicester's famous May and October cheese fairs. Like Stilton, it quickly became popular in the capital and by the mid-eighteenth century was a firm favourite.

These days, food dye rather than carrots creates Red Leicester's distinct orange colour, but the cheese still maintains its mellow flavour. Only two dairies in Leicestershire produce the traditional variety of Red Leicester, one being Sparkenhoe Farm at Upton near Market Bosworth.

PIES AND SNACKS

The Melton Mowbray Pork Pie was actually a by-product of Leicestershire's cheese industry. Whey left over from cheese making was a perfect pig food. This encouraged the people of Melton Mowbray in particular to keep them as livestock.

The abundance of pork made it a staple food for labourers. The meat was made into the perfect portable packed lunch by baking it in a disposable pastry pot.

By the late eighteenth century, fox hunting was an integral part of Melton country life and the local landed gentry became curious about the pies consumed by their grooms and servants.

And so the pork pie went mainstream. The local huntsmen began to buy them from shops in Melton town. In 1831, enterprising Melton baker, Edward Adcock, having noted that the local gentry were lapping the pies up, decided to market them in London.

Soon, demand was such that other businesses were following suit. The hot water crust pastry, which was originally little more than a disposable wrapping, became an integral part of the dish.

It was shaped around a bottle or wooden dolly, before the filling of uncured pork and bone stock jelly was packed in.

Today the pork pie continues to be made around Melton: hand formed and from uncured meat. Ye Olde Pork Pie Shoppe in Melton Mowbray was established in 1851. Now owned by Dickinson & Morris, it is the last firm in Melton to bake authentic pork pies on the premises. Like Stilton, the Melton Mowbray pork pie has been granted protected status by the EU.

But while its adoption by the landed gentry ensured its national fame, the pork pie is still a Leicestershire favourite – traditionally for Christmas Day breakfast!

Pies in general seem to be popular in Leicestershire. In 1963, Trevor Storer began selling pies made to his wife's own recipes to chip shops and football stadiums.

Trevor's pies became a firm and lucrative favourite, leading him to set up a factory for mass production and renaming his company Pukka Pies Ltd. Some sixty million pies are made daily at the company's Leicester factory, which employs 360 local people.

The pork pie is not the only Leicestershire favourite to evolve through necessity. Walkers Crisps were produced by the local butchers, the Walker family, whose business was established in Leicester in the 1880s. Meat rationing in the Second World War saw trade drop, so Walkers looked for alternative ways to make money by tapping into the rising popularity of potato crisps as a popular snack. Around 50 per cent of all British crisps are now produced under the Walkers brand at their factory in Leicester.

CAKES AND SWEETS

Whetstone Cakes are a Leicestershire specialty made with caraway seeds and rosewater. The recipe was first recorded in 1741.

Older still is the Bosworth Jumble biscuit, reputedly baked for Richard III to take to the Battle of Bosworth. The dough was made from butter, sugar, eggs and flour and flavoured with either caraway seed, aniseed or almond before being shaped into a knot and boiled before baking.

Richard lost the battle and the cakes – which were reputedly liberated and eaten by his rival Henry Tudor. From then onwards the jumbles were baked in an 'S' shape in honour of the victor – using the recipe found in the dead hand of Richard's own cook.

'Jumble' comes from the Latin for twin, *gemmel*, which explains the cake's symmetrical shape rather better than the defeat of one king by another!

Leicestershire also has its own form of cheesecake, although they are not recognised as such by the rest of the country.

Leicestershire cheesecakes are small pastry tarts filled with sweetened curd cheese and dried fruit. The tarts could well have been made as early as the Middle Ages, as the accounts of Eleanor, Countess of Leicester and wife of Simon de Montfort, mentions 'cheese in tarts'. Nowadays, the cakes have to be marketed as curd cakes to avoid confusion with the more traditional cheesecake with the biscuit base. But Leicestershire locals stubbornly refuse to refer to them as such. To them, the little tarts are the definitive cheesecakes.

Sand Cake is another traditional Leicestershire cake. Loaf shaped, they are made from a mix of wheat flour and either cornflour or potato flour to give them the sandy texture that earns them their name. Sometimes served topped with a lemon icing, the Sand Cake used to be a favourite for dessert, especially when served with fruit and cream.

A Leicester grocer developed Fox's Glacier Mints in the late nineteenth century. Walter Fox originally established the company in a Leicester warehouse in 1880. In 1918, the famous mints were first developed: clear, minty and in the ice cube shape that remains popular today.

The trademark of the mints was Peppy the polar bear. Local artist and illustrator of the Thomas the Tank Engine books, Clarence Reginald Dalby, designed the famous polar bear motif.

THE ORIGINS OF AFTERNOON TEA

While visiting Belvoir Castle in the 1840s, Anna Russell, Duchess of Bedford, found that the time between luncheon at midday and dinner at 8 p.m. left her feeling extremely peckish in the afternoon.

So, to avoid offending her hosts, the duchess had servants sneak her up some tea with bread and butter at mid-afternoon to sustain her between meals. She continued this secret ritual even after her stay at Belvoir Castle ended, inviting other lady guests to join her at her country house, Woburn Abbey. This 'small and select' group of afternoon diners gathered in the duchess's rooms, tempted by the tea, which had developed to include small sandwiches and cakes.

The ladies and the duchess herself took their new, illicit habit back to London, where it was openly served. Afternoon tea quickly became an established practice – in middle- and upper-class houses at least.

CAPTAIN SCOTT'S EXPEDITION

In 1901, Market Harborough company W. Symington supplied Captain Scott's ill-fated Antarctic expedition with its dried goods of pea flour and pea soup. Fifty years later, one of the expedition's food stores was rediscovered – and Symington's pea flour was still in perfect condition.

MILLS

Claybrooke Mill in Claybrooke Magna is one of the only commercial watermills in Leicestershire still producing flour. The current mill dates to 1723 but milling has taken place on the site for the last 1,000 years. Today, Claybrooke produces a range of traditional and modern flours, such as Stonechat Flour and a chilli flour mix.

TERMS FOR FOOD

Leicestershire folk have their own particular names for many everyday types of food and drink. Here's just a few examples:

Bungole – cheese
Rocks – sweets
Oakey – ice cream
Council pop – tap water

Cob – roll or bap
Guzgogs – gooseberries
Snaps – lunch
Toggly – buttered toast

CURRY

The first curry restaurant in Leicestershire, The Taj Mahal, was founded on Highfield Street, Leicester, in 1960.

Its owner, Noor Ahmed, had moved to the city just after the Second World War. He found himself one of only twenty Asians in the whole city. From the start, his restaurant depended on enticing English diners, as well as giving his expatriate friends a taste of home.

The last owner of the restaurant, Ali Ashraf, remembers the initial English reaction to this new, exotic food. 'People were very scared it would be very hot,' he said.

But clearly they liked it, for curry took off in a big way across the whole county. In 2007, Leicester was declared the curry capital of Britain, with Belgrave Road the place for a real Leicester curry. The Taj Mahal itself remained open for fifty-five years before its sad closure in 2015.

Curry has also married itself with more traditional Leicester food. McIndians, established in 1989 with its cheeky byline 'You've tried the cowboys, now try the Indians', have spiced up traditional takeaway favourites such as burgers and fish and chips.

Asian food in Leicestershire is big business for more than just restaurants. Fifteen major Indian food manufacturers are located in the county. The Leicester Bakery Ltd is one of the largest specialist bread producers in the UK – commercially producing naan and pitta breads. Founded in 1977 by Mohamed Sabat to sell pitta bread across the Midlands, in 1984 it expanded its operations to launch handmade naans and chapattis.

BELGRAVE'S GOLDEN MILE

For a truly unique experience of Asia within Leicestershire, a visit to Leicester's Golden Mile along Belgrave Road is a must. Vibrant and full of the sounds and smells of another continent, the first Asian shops began to open in the early 1970s. One of the first was an Asian supermarket called Upkar, which specialised in selling Asian fruits and vegetables.

But there is much more to Leicestershire's world food than just curry. Tapas, Italian, Chinese, Greek, Arabic, French and Afro-Caribbean cuisine are all represented – especially in the city of Leicester where its world-famous market sells all the ingredients you need to prepare your own delicious dishes.

BILTONG AND BANGERS

W. Archer & Sons, butchers on Queens Road, Leicester, have developed a new Leicestershire favourite: South African biltong.

Biltong is high in protein and low in carbs – which explains why Archer's version is so popular with local sportsmen as well as the South African ex-pats – one of whom was the inspiration for the butcher's venture. 'An Afrikaans student came in one day, about four years ago, and said he wanted some beef to make his own biltong at home,' explained owner Sean in an interview with the *Leicester Mercury*. 'He made me some and I thought it would be great to start making my own and selling it in the shop.'

In fact, so good are Archer's South African goodies that ex-Leicester Tigers and England player Dan Hipkiss still received weekly 2kg dehydrated deliveries of his favourite biltong when he moved 120 miles away to play for Bath – which he shared with his South African teammates.

MARKETS AND FOOD FESTIVALS

Melton Mowbray has been a market town for over 1,000 years. Recorded as Leicestershire's only market in the 1086 Domesday survey, it is the third oldest market in England. Tuesday has been market day ever since royal approval was given in 1324.

The town itself is known as 'The Rural Capital of Food' and since 2009 has been the host of the British Pie Awards, which celebrates all varieties of British pies – not just the pork pie!

The annual East Midlands Food Festival held in Melton Mowbray attracted over 200 exhibitors and 20,000 visitors in 2007, making it the largest British regional food festival.

Loughborough, Market Harborough and Hinckley also have long-established markets. Market Harborough's has been in service since the early thirteenth century, Hinckley market is 700 years old and Loughborough's 800-year-old market was voted Best Large Outdoor Market of the year in 2017.

Leicester Market is 700 years old. It is the largest covered market in Europe, selling a wide variety of fruit and vegetables from across the world, as well as meat and fish, fresh spices and general haberdashery. It was voted Britain's favourite market in 2011 and has been home to some 300 businesses.

LIQUID REFRESHMENT

BEER

Everards Brewery is the county's largest brewer, producing beers such as the famous Tiger, Old Original and Everards Bitter.

'No effort shall be found wanting in the production and supply of genuine ale of a first-rate quality,' said its founder William Everard in 1849, when he set up the first brewery with Thomas Hull.

By 1892, the company had expanded to Burton on Trent after leasing the Bridge Brewery. The Trent Brewery was leased in 1898 and renamed the Tiger Brewery in 1901 when Everards brought it outright. Today it houses a museum as in 1985, brewing shifted back to Castle Acres in Leicester. Everards is still based in Leicester today. The brewery remains in the Everard family and has 175 pubs about the county.

Other local breweries include:

Belvoir Brewery, Old Dalby
Parish Brewery, Burrough on the Hill
The Pig Pub Brewery, Claybourne Magna
Anstey Ale Brewery, Anstey

NOTABLE PUBS AND HOSTELRIES

The Belper Arms in Newton Burgoland dates back to 1290, when it was known as The Shepherd and Shepherdess Inn. It is the oldest pub in Leicestershire.

The oldest pub in Leicester is The Bowling Green on Oxford Street, which dates to the 1700s. In the 1990s its name was changed to The Polar Bear to commemorate the motif of Fox's Glacier Mints, but recently the pub has reverted back to its original name.

When Henry VIII divorced his fourth wife, a pretty house in Melton Mowbray was gifted to her as part of the settlement. Today it is a pub, The Anne of Cleves, named in honour of its former owner.

The former home of the Everard family became a pub – The Stamford Arms – in 1921. But according to Groby Heritage Group, the tall chimney of the pub used to belong to a quarry.

The Man Within Compass in Whitwick is unique for its name, which is of uncertain origins and not found anywhere else in England. It is known to the locals as The Rag and Mop – for equally obscure reasons.

The Bull Inn at Bottesford was once played host to Laurel and Hardy. Stan Laurel's sister was the landlady, and the comedy duo stayed there in April 1952 while they appeared at the Empire Theatre, Nottingham. Laurel and Hardy returned to the Bull for Christmas 1953, when they happily pulled pints behind the bar for the pub's regulars.

MINERAL WATER

Mineral water is not a modern phenomenon. In the nineteenth century, Leicestershire was well known for its mineral waters – and still produces it to this day.

The Charnwood Hills are a source of exceptionally pure water, which explains why Swithland Spring Water grew up in the area and still flourishes.

But the company is not the area's first producer of mineral water. Whitwick was once home to three mineral water factories, the largest of which, Beckworth and Co. on Cademan Street ran from 1875 to the 1970s. Horace Stinson's enterprise was more short-lived, running only from 1912 to 1928, while Massey's of Castle Street only lasted from 1916 to 1941.

8

SPORT AND LEISURE

SPORT...

COCKFIGHTING

In 1849, cockfighting was declared illegal. Until that point, it was a favourite sport in Leicestershire.

Initially, cockfighting was the preserve of the well-to-do. In 1595, Elizabethan spectators in Leicester laid out 21 shillings and four pence for sweet wine, cherries, cake and bread for the 'gentlemen' spectators. The match in question took place in a purpose-built roofed pit, somewhere between Halford and Granby Streets.

Melton Mowbray also had its own purpose-built pit, just behind the Anne of Cleves public house. So many people would attend during the Croxton Park race week that a new pit was built in 1825 to accommodate 500 spectators.

Another reason that matches were the preserve of the gentry were the huge sums bet at them – sometimes between 50 and 500 guineas. Inter-county matches even occurred. The *Leicester and Nottingham Journal* of 1768 advertised a fight between 'the gentlemen of Leicestershire and the gentlemen of Nottinghamshire, to shew and weigh 21 cocks for the main sand to fight for two guineas a battle'.

'THE BEST HUNTING GROUND IN ENGLAND'

Leicestershire is considered to be the birthplace of fox hunting – so much so that the fox is the county symbol, adorning not only the county council's coat of arms but the emblems of its county cricket club and Leicester City Football Club.

It wasn't until the eighteenth century that fox hunting developed as a sport, rather than a way of culling 'vermin'. Key to its rise was the enclosure of land. At this time, landowners were portioning off open land into smaller, separate fields that were easier to farm. This reduced the open ground available to the deer population, leading to its decline.

Fewer deer meant less deer stalking. So, the landed gentry needed to find another way to amuse themselves. The first man believed to own a pack of foxhounds in England was Thomas Boothby of Tooley Park near Desford, who established his pack in 1696. But the 'father of fox hunting' was Hugo Meynell, who took over from Boothby as Master of the Quorn Hunt in 1753 and remained in post until 1800.

In 1753, when he was 18, Meynell began to experiment with a new breed of hound at his estate of Quorndon Hall. His new hounds were faster and had more stamina. So, to use them to their full potential, Meynell invented a new kind of hunt.

Since the Middle Ages, it had been traditional for hunting to occur in the morning, when foxes and other wild creatures were slowed down by their nightly feed. Meynell wanted more of a challenge for his new breed of dogs – a challenge that would make hunting more exciting (for the hunters at least!). So, he introduced the mid-morning meet. By this time, the fox had digested its nightly meal, making it lighter on its feet and more of a challenge to catch. Fences between the sections of enclosed land added an extra dimension and so the modern hunt was born.

STRANGE SPORTS, PAST AND PRESENT

The Whipping Toms

The custom of the Whipping Toms at Leicester's Shrove Tuesday Fair began as a primitive game of hockey, with two teams of men and boys playing to score in goals at either end of the Newarke. At 1 p.m. the match would end and three men in blue smocks carrying wagon whips and bells would clear the players away.

But by the early nineteenth century the custom had 'evolved'. Instead, at 1 p.m. a bell rang to clear away the patrons of the Shrove Tuesday Fair. Anyone in the know would quit the area very quickly, for if they did not – or they were not prepared to pay a fine of 2*d* (or pad their legs) – they would become victims of the Whipping Toms. For now, instead of hitting a ball, the Toms struck any unlucky trespasser to their area about the legs.

The violence and disorder of the 'game' was such that in 1846 Leicester Corporation obtained an Act of Parliament to bring the 'sport' to an end.

Extreme Ironing

Leicester is the birthplace of a little-known sporting phenomenon: Extreme Ironing, 'the latest danger sport that combines the thrills of an extreme outdoor activity with the satisfaction of a well-pressed shirt' according to the Extreme Ironing Bureau.

In 1997, Leicester resident Phil Shaw was contemplating the drudgery of the mundane chore after a hard day at work and decided to make it more fun by combining it with his passion for rock climbing.

It worked for Phil. Calling himself 'Steam', he began touring in 1999 to promote his new sport. Extreme Ironing is now especially popular in Germany, the USA, New Zealand, Australia, South Africa and Fiji. Participants don't limit themselves to rocks:

activities such as skiing, canoeing, marathon running, sky and scuba diving have been conjoined with the iron and the ironing board.

In 2002, the British team won gold and bronze at the first World Extreme Ironing Championships.

FOOTBALL

In the Middle Ages, football was considered a nuisance game, played in the streets to the inconvenience of all but the players. In 1467 and 1488 it was even outlawed in Leicester by order of its Corporation. The sport's reputation did not improve when, in 1592, players in Oadby were referred to as 'abandoned persons'.

The custom of **bottle-kicking** ever Easter Monday at Hallaton may be a survival of an early form of football. Every year, teams from Hallaton and the neighbouring village of Medbourne gather at Hallaton's 'hare pie bank' for something that is a cross between an impromptu rugby/football match.

Firstly, the hare pie is cut into pieces and distributed among the crowd. Teams then kick two 5kg wooden bottles (in fact small wooden barrels hooped with iron and containing ale) between the village boundaries. Goals are set a mile apart, meaning the resulting scramble occurs over fences, fields and streams. The winner is decided by the best of three bottles, meaning the 'match' could go on all day!

Leicester Fosse Football Club was formed in 1884 by former pupils of Wyggeston School. The fledgling club's first game occurred that same year with a team from Syston. The Fosse won 5–0.

The following year, the burgeoning team established its headquarters on Victoria Park. During this period, the team colours were brown and blue, rather than the familiar white and blue of today.

But as with other Leicester sports, Victoria Park was just a stopping point for the Fosse. In 1887 the club moved to the cycle and cricket ground on Belgrave Road. There they stayed until Leicester Tigers outbid them for the land. But in 1891 the team settled at a new, permanent home at Filbert Street.

The early years of the twentieth century were not successful for the club. They finished bottom of the Second Division of the Football League in 1903/04 and in 1908/09 were relegated from the First Division.

Then, in 1919, the team changed its name. Leicester had just regained its city status. So, Leicester Fosse became Leicester City. Suddenly the newly named team was on the up. In 1949 they reached the FA Cup Final – but lost 3–1 to Wolves. In 1969 the team played in the FA Cup Final for the last time in its history. However, Leicester City's glory days were not over. In 2016 the club won the Premier League for the first time following challengers Tottenham's 2–2 draw with Chelsea.

Leicester City has been the starting point in the careers of several famous footballers, including England player and TV sports commentator Gary Lineker, who began to play for his home team in 1977, turning professional in 1978. One of England's greatest goalkeepers, Peter Shilton, was also born in Leicester and honed his skills at Leicester City.

In 1894, Loughborough Athletic and Football Club won the Midland League, which led to their election into the Football League Second

Division. That same year, according to Julia Skinner, they played a friendly match against 1894/95 FA Cup winners, Aston Villa. Loughborough won 2–1. The man of the match was star player Albert Carnelly. Albert was famous for his cap, which he wore when playing. It was said if he took it off, a goal would be scored.

RUGBY

Leicester Tigers are the most successful English rugby union club since the beginning of the Premiership in 1987.

The club was founded in 1880 along Belgrave Road in Leicester. Their nickname was coined in 1885, from the team's original brown and yellow kit – possibly inspired by the local regiment, who had served in India and who were also known as the Tigers.

The Tigers made various switches in the 1890s. First, they changed home ground, establishing themselves at Welford Road in 1892. The terms of renewal of their new lease at Belgrave Road was unacceptable, so the club agreed terms with Leicester Corporation and signed a ten-year lease on a parcel of land sandwiched between Welford and Aylestone Roads – the site they still occupy today.

The new ground was in a much better position for the club, being nearer the town centre. In all, it cost £1,100 to prepare and the new ground opened in grand style on 10 September 1892. The Tigers's first match at their new home was against the Leicestershire XV. The Tigers won 17–0.

In 1895 the club switched kit, opting for the current scarlet, green and white strip. But they still remained the Tigers.

Three years later the team had their first major win – the 1898 Midlands Counties Cup, which they proceeded to win every year until 1905. The Tigers then dropped out to 'give other teams a chance'!

By the late twentieth century the team was going from strength to strength. Supporter numbers were on the increase and coaches such as Chalkie White ensured that the wins were too. In 1997, six Leicester players were selected to play in the British Lion's tour of South Africa. Between 1998 and 2002 the team won the Premiership title four years in a row, and have won the English Premiership ten times. Leicester were also the first team to win the European Cup successively.

The Tigers won the Heineken Cup in 2001 and 2002, were also European Champions for 2001 and 2002, English Champions from 2000–2002 and 2006–2010, and top of the Rugby Premiership in 2010.

Notable Leicestershire rugby players include:

- Dorian West, MBE – Rugby World Cup winner.
- Martin Johnson, CBE – Captained England to the World Cup in 2003. Played for Leicester Tigers 1989–2005.
- Martin Corry, MBE – 279 appearances for Leicester Tigers and 64 for England.

CRICKET

The first recorded cricket match in Leicestershire occurred in Barrow upon Soar in 1744. In the days before factories, the sport was especially popular with framework knitters who had weekends free to practise the game.

Cricket quickly spread across the county, becoming an important village sport, popular at Hathern, Long Whatton, Shepshed, Loughborough, Hinckley, Lutterworth, Wigston and Fleckney. In Melton Mowbray, the cricket season went on until October every year.

Players began to compete against other clubs – some local, such as Nottingham, with others as far afield as London. Loughborough hosted the first inter-county match against Nottingham, while at Barwell, the annual match against Coventry and North Warwickshire has been played since 1807.

In 1820, the Leicestershire and Rutland Cricket Club was formed, but the club lacked a home ground. Leicester's St Margaret's pasture was initially used for fixtures, followed in 1825 by the Wharf Street ground, which was considered the finest cricket pitch in England. Sadly, the land was sold for building in 1860.

By 1872, the club had relocated to Victoria Park. Many matches were played there but enclosing the cricketing area for games was expensive. A new, permanent home was required.

In 1877, for the sum of £40,000, 16 acres of land were purchased along Aylestone Road. A sports complex was constructed, with an athletics ground, a hotel for visitors and a 12-acre cricket pitch, which took up the lion's share of the space.

The new ground was initially known as 'The Aylestone Ground' but it was quickly renamed Grace Road. Many believe this was after the famous cricketer W.G. Grace, when it was actually after a local landowner.

The first match at the newground was held in summer 1878, between the Leicestershire XI and a visiting Australian team, the 22 Colts. Thirty thousand people – still a record attendance there to this day – watched Leicestershire play the Aussies.

SWIMMING

Jenny Fletcher of Belgrave was known as 'the world's first great woman swimmer'. She was an undefeated swimming champion between 1906 and 1909, setting eleven world records, earning six Champion of England medals and an Olympic gold at the 1912 Games in Stockholm.

BOXING

In the early nineteenth century, boxing was illegal and unregulated. But that did not prevent its popularity – especially among the upper classes. Even the king was a boxing fan!

The first battle for the bareknuckle world boxing title was held near Wymondham in Leicestershire on 28 September 1811 between Tom 'The Moor' Molineaux, a freed slave from America, and Tom Cribb of England.

The choice of venue was cunning, situated as it was on the boundary of Leicestershire, Rutland and Lincolnshire. The match was illegal so – if need be – the 15–20,000 spectators could avoid arrest by the magistrates of one county by crossing over into one of the others – even though many of the spectators were local officials themselves!

The match lasted just twenty minutes, with Cribb winning in the eleventh round by knocking Molineaux unconscious. The winner walked away with the prize of a cup, £2,600 – and a broken jaw.

Notable Leicestershire boxers include:

- Market Harborough's Jack Gardner represented Britain in the 1948 London Olympics, before going on to become British, British Empire and European Heavy Weight Champion.
- Rendall Munroe. Leicester born and based, Munroe was the WBA Interim Super Bantamweight Champion and has also held Commonwealth titles.
- Chris Pyatt. The former World Middleweight Champion boxer may be Islington born but he has made Leicester his home.

HORSE RACING

The first horse race in Leicestershire was recorded at Leicester in 1603 on the Abbey Meadows – the town's first racecourse. The racing conditions were less than ideal. The land was liable to flooding from the nearby River Soar and the races something of a struggle for the

 horses that often had to wade knee deep to the finish line.

So, in 1742, the course moved to St Mary's Field in Leicester's South Fields. However, this too was susceptible to flooding – with the added disadvantage of four turnpike

roads to interrupt the races. Therefore, the races moved to what is now Victoria Park, which was at least dry and open. And there they stayed until 1883, when the sport moved to its current home in Oadby.

FAMOUS RACEHORSES AND THEIR TRAINERS

The 1914 Grand National winner Sunloch was trained in Loughborough. His owner was local man Tom Tyler, who trained the horse behind the Brush Works. Sunloch was a 100-1 outsider – until the locals began to back him, shattering the odds. His win meant the lucky punters of Loughborough raked in £10,000 between them.

The thoroughbred Burrough Hill Lad was named by owner Stan Riley after the Leicester hill and the village of his birth. Trained by Jenny Pitman, he competed in a total of forty-two races, half of which he won, including victories in 1984 at the Cheltenham Gold Cup, Hennessy Gold Cup and King George VI Chase.

Jenny Pitman was herself was born and bred in Leicestershire, and was the first woman to train a Grand National winner, Corbiere, in 1983. Jenny came from a family of horse trainers, married jockey Richard Pitman and established her own point-to-point yard, which became a first-class institution, producing her first win in 1975.

DONINGTON PARK RACING CIRCUIT

The first permanent racing park cicuit in England, Donington Park was established after the First World War by Fred Craner, a motorcycle rider. Craner approached the owner of Donington Hall and persuaded him to allow the use of the roads on the Donington estate for racing.

The first race took place on Whit Monday 1931 on a track that was 2 miles and 327 yards (3,518m) in length. It was such a success that by 1933 Craner had permission to build a permanent trackway.

Once built, the racecourse was used for motor racing. The first race was the Donington Park Trophy Race held on 7 October 1933. The first Donington Grand Prix was in 1935.

The racetrack fell into disuse after it was converted into a military vehicle depot during the Second World War. But in 1971, Tom Wheatcroft brought the land and revived the circuit, and on 28 May 1977, Donington finally reopened.

Since then, the site has hosted both motor racing and speedway events, including the British Touring Car Championship, the British Superbike Championship, the 1993 European Grand Prix and the 2006 World Series. But loss of the rights to host the British Grand Prix and British Superbike Championships has once again led to the track's decline.

Notable Leicestershire racing drivers include Coalville's own speedway rider, Fred Wilkinson, who raced for England against Australia in 1931 and ran Lansdowne Garage in Syston. Formula One driver Roger Williamson was born in Ashby de la Zouch. A British Formula 3 champion, Williamson tragically died during the 1973 Dutch Grand Prix – his second Formula One race.

Ray Wilson is a former international speedway rider, and the son of Leicestershire speedway rider Ron Wilson. Although he was born in Surrey, Ray, who was World Pairs Champion in 1972 and British Speedway Champion in 1973, now calls Leicestershire home.

... AND LEISURE

TRADITIONAL LEICESTERSHIRE FESTIVALS

Yearly Fairs
In the days before cinemas and theatres, fairs provided seasonal bouts of entertainment in Leicestershire. Every town and village held at least one annually. At its peak, Leicester held six.

Fairs were places of food, drink, games and curiosities. Humberstone Gate Fair, which was held every May in Leicester, epitomises their spirit. The *Leicester Journal* described how the site of the fair was originally a piece of waste ground on the south

side of Humberstone Gate. Entrance prices varied according to social standing: 1 shilling for ladies and gentlemen, sixpence for tradesmen and 3 pence for working people.

Animals such as zebras, and the 'kangaroo rat from Botany Bay' were on show, along with sword swallowers, fire-eaters, Irish giants, dwarfs, armless ladies, wrestlers, tumblers, thieves and tricksters. The fair was opened by a proclamation at the High Cross followed by a procession led by the mayor.

When the last fair was held in 1904, the *Leicester Guardian* applauded the end of an 'annoying anachronism that had no place in modern life'. People had better amusements in cinemas, theatres, music halls and libraries, the *Guardian* declared. So, it was goodbye to the fair.

Perhaps it was just as well fairs died off, for they could be dangerous places. Aside from drink-fuelled brawls and pickpockets, the exhibits themselves could turn nasty. During the Elizabethan period, a lion at Loughborough Fair escaped, fatally injuring a local townsman called Nicholas Wollands.

One-Offs
Many fairs and exhibits were once-in-a-lifetime specials, never to be repeated. In Leicestershire they included:

- A two-month exhibition in 1930 of Madame Tussaud's waxworks at Leicester Theatre.
- A visit to Leicester by Buffalo Bill's Wild West Show in August 1891. Billed as a 'Representation of Indian and Frontier Life', which featured genuine cowboys and Indians, the show set up camp on Belgrave Road's cricket and bicycle ground.
- In February 1784, the winter was so severe in Leicester that the River Soar froze solid and a grand masquerade was held on its frozen waters. Thousands of spectators gathered on the riverbanks and along the nearby West Bridge to watch a performance where 'Harlequin, columbine, pantaloons and clown were represented'.

LEICESTERSHIRE WAKES

Wakes were annual fairs held to commemorate the anniversary of the patron saint of the local church. A medieval custom, they reached the pinnacle of their popularity in Leicestershire during the early twentieth century.

The local gentry or employers often funded the wakes. At Bardon, the quarry owner laid on the August wake fair for the local school children. The streets were decorated, and a band and parade opened the event, which culminated in a fair and tea for the village green.

But often wakes were not held at such pleasant times of the year because of the birthday of the church. Whetstone and Ibstock's wakes occurred in October. Instead of bunting, the streets and fairground were lit with naphtha flares to illuminate the dark autumn days.

FESTIVALS TODAY

Modern Leicestershire still keeps many of these old festivals alive, such as the traditional May celebrations held at places like Oadby, while Mayfest is a celebration of the month in general based at Stanford Hall, Lutterworth.

St George's Day celebrations have also recently been revived, especially in Leicester, which marks the occasion with parades and pageants across the city.

Leicester also commemorates its long history with events such as the Castle Park Festival and Riverside Festival. The city also hosts the Leicester Comedy Festival, which has run continuously since 1994, making it the longest running of its kind in the UK.

The county's Asian and Caribbean communities have further enriched Leicestershire's festival culture. Leicester's Caribbean Carnival, held every August since 1985, includes a spectacular procession of floats and musicians who parade through the city centre and Highfields district before culminating in a fair on Victoria Park.

In addition, the city celebrates the Chinese New Year, the Hindu festivals of Holi and Dussehra, the Sikh festival of Vaisakhi and the Jewish festival of Hanukkah. It is also the number one city in the UK to mark the Hindu festival of Navratri, with over 100,000 people taking part. In 2016, Eid was marked with a mass celebration on Victoria Park when thousands of Muslims gathered to celebrate the end of Ramadan.

One of Leicester's most famous festivals is Diwali. The Hindu festival of lights in Leicester is the biggest outside India, with over 30,000 people attending the celebrations. Festivities centre along the city's Golden Mile at Belgrave Road, extending into the city centre itself, where Christmas lights are put up early to mark this festival.

THE SMALL AND LARGE SCREEN

Bollywood in Leicestershire

Leicestershire in the twenty-first century has become a favourite location with Bollywood. In 2001 *Iss Pyaar Ko Kya Naam Doon?* (What Shall I Name This Love?) became the first Bollywood film to be shot entirely on location in Leicester. Most of the sixty extras were locals. This was followed in 2004 by gangster film *Raakh* (Ashes), which had 50 per cent of its scenes shot around the city.

Bollywood's interest in Leicestershire has spread. In 2007, the University of Leicester's botanical gardens and the Grand Union Canal featured in *Samundar Paar* (Overseas), an Indian TV series telling the story of British Asians.

In 2012, the Golden Mile became the city's latest star when it was used as a setting for the comedy *Jadoo*. Written by Leicester-born Amit Gupta, it is the story of two brothers, two restaurants and the ensuing war over the rights to their mother's recipe books. This time, the cast is probably more familiar to the general audience, featuring Madhur Jaffrey and actor Harish Patel of *Run Fatboy Run* fame.

Bollywood aside, Leicestershire is famous for its actors of the small and large screen – Graham Chapman, of Monty Python fame, was born in Leicester, as was Parminder Nagra, who has starred in *Bend It Like Beckham*, *ER* and US crime drama *The Blacklist*. Michael Kitchen of *Foyle's War* is also Leicester born, as is Richard Armitage, star of *Robin Hood*, *Spooks* and *The Hobbit* film trilogy.

Elsewhere in the county, Loughborough has produced David Neilson, the actor best known for portraying Roy Cropper in *Coronation Street*. Actor and director Sir Richard Attenborough grew up in Leicester and cut his acting teeth at Leicester's Little Theatre on Dover Street.

MUSIC

Leicestershire is not short of famous musicians and bands. The rock band Kasabian originate from around the county, with the founder band members meeting at Countesthorpe Community College.

Other local musicians include Phil Oakey of the Human League, David 'Pick' Withers and John Illsley – both of Dire Straits. The 1970s group Showaddywaddy, punk garage band Crazyhead and Frank Benbini of Fun Lovin' Criminals are also all Leicestershire-born.

Local music festivals include Glastonbudget, the biggest tribute festival in the world, which is held at Turnpost Farm, Wymeswold and the Leicester Belgrave Mela, a celebration of South Asian music and dance.

THE TOURIST INDUSTRY

The Home of the Package Tour
Thomas Cook was a cabinetmaker from Market Harborough. He was also a devoted member of the Leicester Temperance Society, whose meetings he diligently walked to after work.

The Midlands County Railway seemed to Cook the perfect way to transport his Leicester brethren to a temperance rally at Southfields Park, Loughborough, so he contacted the railway to organise transport for a large party – a first in itself – before chartering the first privately hired excursion train offered to the general public.

On 5 July 1841, Cook packed 540 temperance campaigners into eight open-air third-class carriages without seats! This was the first ever package tour. Each person paid 1 shilling for their rail fare, and were entertained by a brass band, followed by tea and buns when they reached their destination.

This early endeavour laid the foundation of Thomas Cook & Son. By 1850, Cook had offices along Leicester's Gallowtree Gate and was organising trips all over the world, including excursions to the great exhibition of 1851 and the first escorted trips for British travellers to the USA, the Middle East and Europe.

Sadly, the Thomas Cook company collapsed in September 2019 with more than £1.7 billion of debt.

SPAS

Leicestershire doesn't immediately spring to mind as a spa county, but its many sources of mineral-rich water have made it quite a spa hotspot – both in the past and today.

The Humberstone Gate Spa in Leicester was built in 1787 around a natural chalybeate spring in an attempt to turn Leicester into a spa town. However, the mineral content of the spring was too low, and the venture folded.

The village of Shearsby was famous for the curative properties of its Holy Well that had long been credited with curing skin diseases, rheumatics, sickness and nervous disorders. So, in the first half of the nineteenth century, the well was converted into a spa. But by 1855 the spa had fallen out of favour – probably because it was discovered that the main constituents of the water were just sodium sulphate and sodium chloride!

Ashby de la Zouch did successfully become a spa town and the chief town of north-west Leicestershire – before its success was supplanted by industrial Coalville.

However, many spas in Leicestershire flourish to this day. In the nineteenth century, Sapcote spa enjoyed lofty patronage. It was established in 1806 by John Frewen Turner, who built a bathhouse over the so-called Golden Well along Stanton Road. The spa was equipped with cold and warm baths, and treatments for rheumatics and skin complaints. The whole spa building cost £600 and was visited by Prime Minister George Canning, and the Duke of Wellington.

Today, Leicestershire's star spa doesn't centre around a water source but a former hunting lodge. Award-winning Ragdale Hall Spa lies in the Leicestershire countryside. The spa doesn't have its own mineral-rich water source, but it does offer guests a unique, purpose-built thermal spa and rooftop infinity pool – features that attract not only visitors from the UK but from as far afield as Dubai!

9

RELIGION AND SUPERSTITION

Leicestershire retains many traditions that
preserve some of the old beliefs.

FOLK BELIEFS AND CUSTOMS

Beating the Bounds is an ancient custom that survived well into the nineteenth century. Every year (or every three years in the case of parishes such as St Mary's in Leicester) it was customary for the village to walk its parish boundaries, 'beating' them out with sticks. Young boys played a central role, with the boys themselves being hit at certain designated points.

Many experts believe this ritual corporal punishment was a weak survival of human sacrifice; offerings to the gods that were made at set points along the borders and margins of a settlement to ensure they were well secured from threats.

According to *The Gentleman's Magazine and Historical Chronicle of 1814*, each Easter around Shipley Hill near Cossington, 'lads and lasses of the adjacent villages meet upon Easter Monday yearly to make merry with cakes and ale'.

The locals regarded this custom to be an ancient tradition dating back to Celtic times. Another custom from the nearby Dane Hills was believed to be just as ancient. The hills were once wild countryside, reputedly haunted by the blue-faced hag, Black Annis, who was said to prey on local children.

Annis is probably a misremembrance of the Celtic goddess Anu or Danu, a goddess of fertility and the harvest. This probably explains the strange custom of the Easter Drag hunt, which was first recorded in 1668.

On the morning of each Easter Monday, races and contests were held on the Dane Hills. But at around noon, a dead cat soaked in aniseed was trailed in front of a pack of hounds just in front of Black Annis's bower and then dragged across the Leicestershire countryside, with hounds, hunters and the mayor and his aldermen in hot pursuit. The hunt continued into Leicester itself, right up to the door of the mayor's house. Here the hunt ended in a formal dinner held by the mayor.

The hunts ceased in the nineteenth century, but local people continued to mark the occasion all the same and instead a fair was held on the Dane Hills – at least until the current housing estate was constructed!

May Day Celebrations in Leicestershire underwent something of a renaissance in the nineteenth century, yet they retained the flavour of something older and pre-Christian.

Old songs show how it was common to begin the celebrations on May Eve, with parties going out to the woods at midnight, returning at dawn with branches and plants to weave into garlands. These garlands were placed at the front of village cottages for good luck.

Every village had its version of the May garland, which was based on a hoop lavishly decorated with flowers such as primrose, cowslip and a Leicestershire favourite, the marsh marigold. Some garlands consisted of single hoops. Others were double or triple combinations, worked into a ball known as 'The May Bush'. Whatever the shape or form, inside each garland was at least one May doll.

The garlands, covered in material such as a lace curtain, were carried on sticks or on a flat basket in a procession through the villages. The participants sang songs and asked for gifts – a tame version of sacrifices. The May Bush – and its dolls – were only revealed to those who paid up in food or money. No doubt the doll represented a spring goddess or ancient spirit of regeneration who would only bless those who sacrificed to her.

SACRED STONES

Leicestershire has no stone circles, but it does boast the odd standing stone or two. The Humber Stone, which stood near

Thurmaston, was a huge granite stone 'eight or perhaps ten feet' in height, and 6ft wide, according to *Gentleman's Magazine* – until the owner of the land it occupied decided the stone was in the way of his plough and so broke it up so that only a stump remained.

The stone, which gives its name to the nearby village of Humberstone, has been known variously as the Hoston, Hostin, Holy and Hell Stone. The name 'Hel' has been linked to the Norsemen as Hel was the name for the Norse goddess of the underworld – and the underworld itself. The stone supposedly guarded a cave that was an entrance to the underworld – although no such portal has been found.

But perhaps the Humber Stone did have some power, for the farmer who ordered its destruction went, in six years, from the owner of 120 acres to abject poverty, dying in the workhouse.

Many people believed that the Humber Stone was frequented by the fairies. Another stone with a similar reputation was St John's Stone, which stood on farmland near Leicester Abbey. Local children used to visit the stone each 24 June – Midsummer's Eve or St John's Day. They would dance around the 7ft-high monolith, but ensured they left well before dark to avoid the wrath of the fairies. By 1840, like the Humber Stone, St John's Stone was completely destroyed.

HOLY WELLS

Sketchley Well was famous as a brightener of intellects. Anyone stupid or dull-witted was often advised to 'go to Sketchley' to take the waters, while someone who came out with a sudden witticism was remarked as having 'been to Sketchley'.

The well at Bruntingthorpe went from holy to hotel. It was situated just outside the village, where a spring spouted into a round pit. The taste of the spring was described as salty and brackish, and useless as a drinking source, even for cattle. But when a local boy with a scorbutic ailment bathed in it and was cured, it was converted into a spa in the nineteenth century and today is the location of the Shearsby Bath hotel.

CHURCHES

FLECKNEY CHURCH AND THE FAIRIES

Local superstitions also play their part in the founding of many of Leicestershire's churches. The fairy folk were believed to have had a hand in the location of Fleckney church. When the foundation stones of the church were originally laid at a site a mile outside of the present village, each night the disgruntled supernatural residents dismantled them and threw them in a nearby stream.

The waters of the stream carried the stones for a distance until they became lodged. Eventually, the builders became resigned to circumstance and decided to build where the stones came to rest. Obviously, this was well away from the fairy's domain as the church was this time allowed to stand.

ST NICHOLAS CHURCH: THE OLDEST CHURCH IN LEICESTER

St Nicholas church in Leicester is located at what was the heart of the Roman city – right next door to what is now the Jewry Wall Museum.

Built in AD 880, St Nicholas is Leicester's oldest place of worship. It was also the city's first cathedral – before the Anglo-Saxon Bishopric of Leicester passed to Lincoln in the eleventh century. Originally, the church was built from masonry scavenged from the abandoned Roman baths next door. Later, the Normans embellished it, and later still the niche in the canopy of the north aisle was added – a remnant from William Wyggeston's original hospital.

The church is a survivor, withstanding Viking attacks and the brutal redevelopment of Leicester in the 1960s when much of the city's medieval past was destroyed.

THE CHURCH THAT DIED OF SHAME

St Mary in Arden in Market Harborough had a bad reputation. Its churchmen were disreputable and the church itself was a bastion of clandestine marriages.

Eventually, in 1650, its privileges were annulled. The church felt the shame of this fall from grace so keenly that reputedly its tower followed suit, crashing down and destroying the main body of the church.

FRISBY ON THE WREAK:
THE GRETNA GREEN OF THE MIDLANDS

The church of St Thomas of Canterbury in Frisby on the Wreake had a similar reputation to St Mary's, although it seems to have managed to remain intact. Between 1756 and 1796, the Revd William Brecknock Wragg was its vicar. The Revd Wragg happily did away with the banns and married any couple on demand, making Frisby a quick stop point for couples eager to be wed. Wragg even married one couple in the parlour of the village inn!

Weddings during the reverend's tenure went up from three or four a year to ten a year. The parish records indicate a large portion of the marriages were between persons from distant parishes who were clearly marrying at Frisby because of the relaxed rules.

However, the law caught up with the obliging vicar. Wragg was tried and sentenced to fourteen years' transportation – a sentence that was set aside because of his advancing old age. So he was defrocked instead.

BEEBY TUB

Beeby tub without a pub, a church without a spire
Two brothers fought and broke their necks
and so 'twas built no higher.

The stubby spire – and unusual name – of the church at the village of Beeby is explained by a sad tale. Two brothers were engaged by the Abbot of Leicester to build a church at nearby Queniborough. The spire of this church was magnificent, visible for miles around, and the Abbot of Croyland and owner of the Manor of Beeby became jealous. He decided his church must be similarly endowed. So he asked for the names of the two masons.

But whereas the build at Queniborough went off without a hitch, work at Beeby was anything but harmonious. The brothers could not agree on the design, and money for the build was short, adding to the tension.

Eventually the tower was built – all but for the spire. The brothers again began to argue – on top of the church – about whether the tower would take the spire's weight. Words turned to blows and such was the ferocity of the fight that they plunged to the ground – onto the very stones that were to build the disputed spire.

To this day the tower remains incomplete – with only a stub instead of a spire.

THE ABBEY OF ST MARY DE PRATIS

The Abbey of St Mary de Pratis, known as Leicester Abbey, was founded in 1143 by the 2nd Earl of Leicester, Robert de Beaumont. It was the wealthiest religious establishment in Leicestershire, as well as one of the largest Augustinian abbeys in England and the place of death of the unfortunate Cardinal Wolsey.

The abbey survived until 1538, largely due to its final abbot, Bourchier, who was installed by Cromwell to ensure a smooth

dissolution. Nonetheless, Bourchier did his best to save the abbey, persuading its canons to accept the king as head of the Church of England, and making gifts to Cromwell. But it was all in vain, and on 28 August 1538 the abbey was finally surrendered.

TWYCROSS CHURCH

Twycross church's thirteenth-century east window is thought to be the oldest stained-glass window in England. However, the window didn't originate in Leicestershire. Instead, it reached its final destination by a rather convoluted route.

The window originated in the Sainte-Chapelle, Paris, from where it was transported during the French Revolution for safe-keeping in England. But it never made it home. Instead, it was presented as a gift to George III and inherited by William IV, who in turn passed it on to Earl Howe, who installed it in Twycross.

THE SMALLEST CHURCH IN LEICESTERSHIRE

Snibston is home to the twelfth-century St Mary's church, the smallest church in Leicestershire that is still in use. Despite having capacity for only thirty worshippers, regular weekly worship still occurs there.

MOUNT ST BERNARD ABBEY

Founded in 1835, Mount St Bernard Abbey near Coalville was the first permanent monastery founded in England since the Reformation. Dedicated to the Cistercian Order, it is also the only Trappist monastery in England.

Its original monks fled France after the French Revolutions of the late eighteenth century and 1830s. Their intended destination was Canada but after a brief stopover in Ireland, they eventually found their way to north-west Leicestershire.

The monks initially lived in a four-room cottage until the monastery, designed by Augustus Pugin, was completed in 1844.

Mount St Bernard has played host to a variety of famous visitors: William Wordsworth visited in 1841 and other visitors included Florence Nightingale and the Pre-Raphaelite Edward Burne-Jones, who wrote in his later years how: 'More and more my heart is pining for that monastery in the Charnwood Forest. Why there? I don't know, only that I saw it when I was little and have hankered after it ever since.'

The monks farmed the land about the abbey but also did a great deal to alleviate the poverty of the local people. The Great Famine in Ireland led to a major influx of Irish immigrants to the area. In 1845, Mount St Bernard gave refuge to 2,788 people, while another 18,887 were given food.

In 1847, a further '36,000 people received charity and hospitality from the hands of the monks', according to the *Catholic Institute Magazine*. In the 1850s a reformatory for young Catholic delinquents was also established. This charity work continued after the Leicestershire coalfield suffered a depression in the 1870s and also during the General Strike of 1926.

In 2009 the abbey was used as the site for the re-interment of 600 medieval Trappist monks excavated from the former site of

Stratford Langthorne Abbey in London that was excavated as part of the extension of the Jubilee line.

Mount St Bernard was proposed as a temporary resting site for the bones of Richard III before his reburial in Leicester Cathedral, but the University of Leicester refused to release the bones.

SAINTS, MARTYRS, DISSENTERS AND HERETICS

EARLY CHRISTIAN MARTYRS IN LEICESTER?

Leicestershire may be able to date its Christianity to pagan times if Andrew Breeze, a lecturer at the University of Navarra in Spain, is correct. Dr Breeze believes that two early Christian martyrs, killed in Roman Britain sometime in the third-century AD, could have met their deaths in Leicester.

The men are two of three Christians recorded by the Venerable Bede as being put to death in Roman Britain. The two men – Aaron and Julius – apparently died at 'the city of the legions'. Many historians believe this is a reference to Caerleon in Wales, but Dr Breeze, referring to the writings of Gildas, says the monk's writings point out the martyrs were buried in lands under Anglo-Saxon rule – ruling out the Welsh town. The only other choice for an applicable city of the legions is Leicester.

ST WISTAN

The ninth-century heir to the Kingdom of Mercia, Wistan, was a pious young man more interested in the religious life than the throne. However, Wistan's cousin, Brifardus, was keen to be king and so plotted his cousin's murder.

Brifardus invited Wistan to an assembly on 1 June near the River Sence in Leicestershire, close to the village of Wistow. Here, he struck down Wistan with the hilt of his sword, after which one of his men stabbed the king in the back.

Wistan's corpse was buried at Repton in Derbyshire, then the capital of Mercia. But the site of his murder developed a reputation for strange sights and miracles. A column of light was seen ascending to heaven and every year on 1 June, human hair sprouted from the ground at the spot where his head hit the ground.

These miraculous occurrences convinced people of Wistan's sainthood and drove Brifardus mad. Meanwhile, a shrine and a church were built near the site of the saint's death, and a village grew up that became known as Wistanstowe – the holy place of Wistan – later shortened to Wistow.

Wistow became a place of pilgrimage, and in 1167 the Archbishop of Canterbury made a pilgrimage there. He, the Abbot of Leicester and other notables all witnessed the hairy growth from the martyr's murder site, which they observed disappeared within the hour.

HUGH LATIMER

Although not a Catholic saint, Hugh Latimer was one of the three Oxford Martyrs of Anglicanism.

Born at Thurcaston in the late fifteenth century, Latimer studied at Cambridge and was ordained as a priest around 1510. He was one of the earliest Protestant reformers and gained royal

favour by supporting Henry VIII's efforts to annul his first marriage to Catherine of Aragon.

Thus his rise to power began. Latimer became Bishop of Worcester and chaplain to the boy king Edward VI.

But it all went wrong when Edwards's Catholic sister, Mary, ascended the throne. In 1553 Latimer was arrested on charges of treason. He was tried in Oxford and burned at the stake on 16 October 1555.

THE LOLLARDS

The term 'Lollard' comes from the Dutch for a murmurer or babbler of prayers. But it acquired a more dangerous meaning in medieval England, being applied to heretics who rejected much of the pomp of the high church, disdaining adornments, money and unnecessary ceremony in religion.

Leicestershire seemed to have a particular affinity with this dissenting religion and was an early centre for its nurture. The Earl of Leicester, John of Gaunt, allowed practising Lollard clerics such as John Wycliffe to exist under his protection. Wycliffe became rector of Lutterworth parish church, a post he held between 1374 and 1384. It was while in Lutterworth that he first translated the Bible into English.

Meanwhile, ordinary people were also taking the lead. A certain William, a smith of Leicester, was one noted case. Self-educated, Smith became a Lollard, abstaining from meat and alcohol. He held meetings at the chapel of St John the Baptist in Leicester, where he set up his headquarters.

Smith garnered considerable support in the town, probably because he advocated that the people should have the right to hold to account those lords and clergy who were 'evildoers'. He also maintained that collective prayer was useless, as was paying for prayers. All that was required of Christians was to live a good life. This essentially was the same as saying the clergy was redundant.

Henry of Knighton records that in the event of running out of firewood for cooking at his headquarters, Smith and a companion took an old wooden image of St Catherine from the chapel and used it for firewood, joking that they were martyring the saint for a second time.

Considering all of this, it was no surprise when at the end of October 1389, the Archbishop of Canterbury, William Courtenay, arrived at Leicester Abbey to deal with the Lollard problem. On 1 November he called William Smith and seven others to an ecclesiastic court to answer the charge of Lollardy.

Instead, the men absconded and so were excommunicated in their absence. But as the sympathetic folk of Leicester were shielding the Lollards, Courtenay placed the whole town under an interdict. Until the fugitives were betrayed or gave themselves up, no church services were held, and the sacraments were denied to the dying.

But Lollardy continued, and not just in Leicester. In the fifteenth century, a William Trivet of Twyford was convicted of being a Lollard and whipped seven times around St Martin's church in Leicester and once around the marketplace.

THE BURNING OF THOMAS MOORE

The reign of Mary I was a dangerous time for those of a reforming nature after the queen tried to zealously re-establish Catholicism across the country.

In April 1556, 24-year-old Thomas Moore was visiting a church in Leicester with some friends. During the visit, Moore was unwise enough to voice some of his more reforming religious opinions, remarking that the statues of the saints were mere empty idols, as was the Eucharist.

An eavesdropper duly reported Thomas and he was summoned to appear in St Margaret's church before the Bishop of Lincoln, Dr John White. At this trial, the bishop tested him. He placed a pyx – a box containing the sacramental wafer – on the altar of the church and asked Thomas what he saw before him. Thomas replied that he saw only ornaments. The bishop then asked if the 'blood, flesh and bones' of Christ were not in the little box? Moore replied no and thus doomed himself. He was found guilty of heresy.

He refused to recant his beliefs and so on 26 June 1556, he was burnt at the stake.

GEORGE FOX AND THE QUAKERS

In 1667, the Society of Friends or Quakers took on the form we recognise today due to the beliefs and efforts of George Fox, a weaver's son from Fenny Drayton.

Fox was a serious young man who disdained luxury and indulgence. For years, he pondered the religious questions that troubled him and after a lengthy study of the Bible, he began to formulate his own religious beliefs. Fox rejected ritual and group prayer, believing salvation lay in a person's heart. He rejected church worship, believing god should be communed with in the open air, and even held the view that women and children could minister.

In 1647, Fox began preaching. One of his first addresses was at Sutton in the Elms outside the parish church. It was at this point that he began to gather a group of like-minded individuals or 'friends', who formed the beginnings of the Quakers.

A local story tells how, in 1662, Fox and some friends were arrested at Swannington and committed to Leicester gaol. There they continued to hold their prayer meetings – until the gaoler tried to break them up by setting his mastiff on them. But the dog was well disposed towards the Quakers and instead, when its master raised his staff to strike the prisoners, the dog seized it and ran off with it to play.

JOHN WESLEY

The founder of Methodism was a frequent visitor to Leicestershire. On 31 July 1770 he lodged at a house in St Nicholas Street, Leicester, as he planned a series of sermons in the town.

Described as a short man, with long white hair and black clothing, Wesley's speech, in the yard of Leicester Castle, was initially rained off and postponed until 5 a.m. the following morning at a house on Millstone Lane, which was a common meeting place for his followers.

Markfield has close links with the Methodist movement and, according to a blue plaque on the church, John Wesley paid thirteen visits to the village. He was allowed to preach in the parish church, but his visits became so popular that he had to accommodate larger crowds by preaching on the village green.

WITCHCRAFT

The belief in witchcraft continued widely in Leicestershire up until relatively recently. According to an Elmesthorpe farmer in 1811:

> It is common almost everywhere amongst the women that when they brew they make crosses to keep the witch out of the mash-

tub, so that the ale might be fine ... farmers and common folk were very great believers in old popular tales of ghost, fairies and witches and of people and cattle being under the evil tongue.

Cases of witchcraft in Leicestershire can be traced back to the Middle Ages. In 1326, a Robert le Mareschal was charged and hanged for the crime of attempting to kill Edward II by witchcraft.

Even the clergy were suspect. On 3 December 1440, the Bishop of Lincoln, Bishop Alnwick, arrived at Leicester to investigate accusations of sorcery against Abbot Sadyngton of Leicester Abbey. The abbot had been investigating a sum of stolen money and when no one confessed, he turned to sorcery. His accusers stated he had taken a young boy to Ingarsby Grange and after murmuring incantations, anointed his thumbnail and bid the boy scry to find the culprit. As a result, a Thomas Ansty, the cathedral canon, was accused of the theft.

The abbot was disliked by his brethren, which probably accounts for the accusation. Perhaps this was why the bishop was lenient and simply allowed Abbot Sadyngton to purge himself of the crime.

But it was after the reformation that Leicestershire's major witch trials began.

JAMES I AND THE WITCHES OF LEICESTER

In 1603, James VI of Scotland ascended the English throne to become James I of England. James had an interest in witchcraft. His ideas seem to have infected his subjects because a series of trials began across the country.

A case that James himself took an interest in and could be said to have solved was that of the bewitching of 12-year-old John Smythe of Husbands Bosworth in 1616. John claimed to be in the thrall of a group of witches who possessed him with their animal familiars. Nine women were arrested and in July 1616 were put on trial.

The women were tried over several days, with John appearing in court to offer the judges first-hand evidence of the 'strange fits' brought about by their magic. Robert Herrick described the evidence to his brother Sir William in a letter:

'Sir Henry Gastings hath done what he could to hold him in his fit but he and another as strong as he could not hold him,' said Hastings. 'If he [John] might have his arm at liberty, he would strike himself such blows on his breast ... that you might hear the sound of it the length of the chamber ... and yet all he did to himself did him no hurt ... 6 of the witches had 6 several spirits-one in the likeness of a horse, another a dog, another a cat, another a fullemer, another a fish, another a cock with whom everyone of them tormented him … when the horse tormented him he would whinny, when the cat tormented him he would cry like a cat. When he was in his fit, they would sometimes brought to him and then they were charged to speak certain words and to name their spirits and one of them speak to another as thus.

The women were found guilty and hanged. But some months later, the king himself was in Leicester and, intrigued by the case, took the opportunity to question John Smythe about his unpleasant experience. The boy, perhaps awed by the king, crumbled and admitted he had made the whole story up.

THE WITCHES OF BELVOIR CASTLE

A few years later, in 1618, the sixth Earl of Rutland, Francis Manners, lord of Belvoir Castle and friend to the king, was himself troubled by witchcraft.

Francis was unlucky with his wives and children. His first wife died in 1608 and after his remarriage, his son and heir Henry died, quickly followed by his second son Francis.

Both the earl and his second wife believed the deaths to be caused by witchcraft. They laid the crime firmly at the door of three former servants: Joan Flowers and her daughters Philippa and Margaret. Their masters had become dissatisfied with the women's work and their opinion of them became very low. Philippa was described as 'lewdly transported with the love of one Thomas Simpson' and Joan described as 'a monstrous, malicious woman, full of oaths, curses and imprecations, irreligious and for anything they saw by her, a plain atheist'.

All three had been sacked, with Margaret the only one offered a pay-off of 40 shillings, a pillow and a mattress of wool. Joan, angry at her treatment, was said to have placed a curse on her former employers. Soon afterwards, the earl and countess became ill with vomiting and convulsions and Henry and Francis died.

The earl ordered the women's arrest and they were taken to Lincoln for questioning, where Joan was accused of murder and her daughters of being accomplices. To prove her innocence, Joan asked for bread and butter, saying if she was guilty 'let it never pass through her'. Minutes after biting into the bread, she died.

Philippa and Margaret admitted to witchcraft. According to their testimony, they had communed with spirits through their familiar, a cat called Rutterkin. Margaret described how Henry was killed. She claimed to have stolen one of his gloves and passed it to Joan, who stroked Rutterkin with it before dipping it in hot water and pricking it. To prevent any further heirs, the women also stole feathers from the earl's bed and a pair of gloves, which they boiled in water and blood.

In the course of the investigation, the Flowers also implicated Anne Baker of Bottesford, Joan Willimot of Goadby and Ellen Greene of Stathorne, stating they were witches who helped them in their vendetta against the earl.

Although no action was taken against these three women, Margaret and Philippa were convicted by their own words and hanged. It is likely that Joan was throttled rather than choking on a condemning bit of bread. Philippa and Margaret were probably tortured into their confessions – or may even have fallen for an offer of leniency. Either way, justice was seen to be done.

THE LAST INDICTMENT FOR WITCHCRAFT

A hundred years later, Leicestershire was the last recorded place in the UK where an accused witch was 'swum' and indicted for witchcraft in a secular court.

On 4 August 1717, twenty-five people appeared at Leicester Assizes to bear witness against Jane Clarke of Wigston Magna and her son and daughter, Joseph and Mary, who were charged with cursing members of the village.

The trio were specifically charged with bewitching a Mary Hatchings to death while tormenting others with illness by 'twisting and distorting of their limbs backwards and forwards' and appearing to their victims at night 'in their own and other shapes'.

A church minister was unable to help the victims, so a local cunning man was called in, who identified a curse. The urine of the victims was sealed in a bottle and then heated in fire. If the urine remained in the bottle, the cunning man explained, all was well, but if it came out then the afflicted remained cursed. When the urine was set to boil, the witches supposedly came into the room, as a cat or a dog or as themselves. They sat on the chimney shaking their fists at the bewitched and grinning in a threatening manner before vanishing up the chimney.

The cunning man completed the cure with a balm of rosemary and marigold in boiled ale and blood rubbed onto the victims' chests. The blood was that of the victim – but the witches' blood was required too.

To acquire the blood, the villagers pursued the three Clarkes and bled them. But they also decided to take the opportunity to acquire evidence for the authorities – using tried and tested measures. Firstly, the witches were 'swum':

> their thumbs and great toes tyed fast together and were thrown
> so bound into the water [where] tho they strove and used all
> endeavours to sink yet they all swam like a corke or an empty barrel.

As all three accused witches floated, they were brought before the assizes. Other evidence presented to the court included bits of stone, dirt and thatch reportedly voided from the victim's bodies. Mary Hatchings also had teeth marks, some human, some dog-like, which were attributed to Mary and Joseph rather than their elderly mother.

Even though the common people still believed in witchcraft, the authorities did not and there were no more witch trials in Leicester.

THE WITCH OF ASTON

But the accusations still came. In June 1776, an old woman of 80 from Aston was accused of bewitching a woman in neighbouring Earl Shilton.

According to the *Leicester and Nottingham Chronicle*, the supposed victim of the curse had suffered for some years from a mark resembling the bite of a tarantula. On 20 June, the woman's husband and her soldier son set upon the old lady, threatening her and held her at sword point, demanding blood from her body and a blessing to remove the curse.

The old lady complied but the 'cure' did not work. So, on 24 June, a group of local vigilantes raised by the supposed victim's family pretended to have a warrant and threw the old lady into a horse pond 'with uncommon brutality'. Fortunately, the woman escaped with her life, despite sinking below the water.

After these events, however, it was the mob that were at risk of indictment, not the accused witch, for the *Chronicle* went on to call for the local magistrates to 'exert themselves to bring to punishment these atrocious offenders'.

WITCHES OF LEICESTER AND THE HIGHCROSS

Today, Leicestershire's witches are the winners. In 2007, the *Telegraph* reported that a local coven was protesting about the name of Leicester's new shopping complex. The proposed name was the Highcross Quarter – to commemorate Leicester's old high cross. But the witches felt this was a misuse of a term used for festivals of the Wiccan calendar.

Rather than use magic, the witches turned to the power of the internet, staking their claim to the name through domain names. But maybe stranger powers were afoot. After trying to buy up the names, and then threatening to take the witches to the United Nations' World Intellectual Property Organization, the developers inexplicably dropped their claim, opting for the name 'Highcross Leicester' instead.

RELIGION TODAY

Today, Leicestershire's religious composition is the most diverse it has ever been – largely because of the make-up of the population of the city of Leicester. The 2011 census shows that while 32.40 per cent of people in the city were nominally Christian, 22.82 per cent had no religion, 18.63 per cent were Muslim, 15.19 per cent were Hindu, 4.38 per cent were Sikh, 0.56 other, 0.37 per cent Buddhist, and 0.09 per cent Jewish. Finally, 5.56 did not state their religion.

The first Hindu temple in Leicester opened in 1969, while the Jain Centre opened as the first consecrated Jain Temple in the Western world. A Hindu sect, the Jains established themselves in Leicester by converting a former Victorian congregational chapel. Marble and stone were laid over the plain Victorian brickwork to create a facade of gods and goddesses.

10

INVASION, CONQUEST, WAR AND REBELLION

ROMANS, BRITONS, SAXONS, VIKINGS

BOUDICA'S DEFEAT

No one really knows where the iconic queen Boudica made her last stand against the Roman invaders, but one possible site lies in Leicestershire. Kevin K. Carroll has suggested that the junction between Watling Street and Fosse Way at High Cross is a likely contender as it would have been the perfect spot for the Second Legion Augusta to move up from Exeter to join the rest of Governor Gaius Suetonius Paulinus's forces at the final, decisive battle for ancient Britain.

AETHELFLEDA THE LIBERATOR

In AD 868, the Vikings invaded Leicestershire, part of a concerted Norse/Danish campaign to capture England. Viking long-ships swarmed down the River Soar, with the city of Leicester in their sights.

These forces overwhelmed and conquered Leicester, destroying some of its old Roman defences, while the rest of the Leicestershire countryside was dealt with in typical Viking style, with sites like Breedon monastery pillaged and destroyed.

By AD 874, Mercia – of which Leicestershire was just a small part – was firmly in Norse hands. The war of conquest was not yet over but a stalemate had been reached. In AD 886, in an attempt to prevent further bloodshed, the extent of Danish territory was agreed by a treaty between Alfred the Great and Guthrum, King of the Danes. Known as the Danelaw, it made Mercia – and by default Leicestershire – a Scandinavian county of England – at least for a while.

But Alfred's daughter, Aethelfleda, had no truck with the treaty. By AD 911, she was Lady of Mercia in her own right after the death of her husband, Aethelred. So, Aethelfleda made it her mission to rid Mercia of the Danes. In AD 918 she liberated Leicester, after her reputation and the sheer strength of her forces caused the Danish to quit the town and relinquish it without a fight.

To ensure security, Aethelfleda refortified Leicester and reputedly built its first castle.

MEDIEVAL MADNESS

THE NORMAN CONQUEST

After the Battle of Hastings in 1066, the Norman consolidation of power across England didn't go quite as smoothly as they had hoped. In Leicestershire, a descendant of one of the county's previous Danish interlopers put up quite a show of resistance to the new invaders.

Eric the Forester was a descendant of a Danish chief called Ericke, who invaded England at the time of King Alfred. Eric was a great landowner – and he wasn't about to relinquish any power to the Norman invaders. So he raised an army from his estates in Leicestershire and made a last stand.

Eric's forces held off the Norman army at Copt Oak near Ulverscroft for some time. He was ultimately defeated and lost his lands anyway. But William the Conqueror so admired his efforts that he spared Eric's life. He also awarded Eric with special office, giving him the command of the royal forces. Eventually, William allowed Eric to retire to his own house in Leicestershire.

The Herrick family are reputedly his descendants.

ANARCHY IN THE UK

In the twelfth century, Princess Matilda was declared heir to the throne of England by her father, Henry I. However, the English barons did not support Henry's choice of queen. And so in 1135, when Henry died, they shifted their allegiance to the king's nephew, Stephen.

With the support of her illegitimate half-brother the Earl of Gloucester, Matilda began a bitter war for the crown with Stephen. So began a nineteen-year period of civil war known as 'The Anarchy', when England fought against itself.

Leicestershire's earl, Robert de Beaumont, was a supporter of the new king and so Leicestershire no doubt was a target for the enraged queen's forces. Shilton Hill was fortified by the earl to defend the main roads crossing the county.

But it was at Leicester Castle that peace was effectively made. The barons of both armies began to meet in secret to make private treaties that would force Stephen and Matilda, and her son Henry, to come to terms. Robert Beaumont was chief amongst the earls who led the peace process, having switched allegiance to Henry in May 1153, and celebrated Pentecost with him at Leicester Castle the following month. The negotiations culminated in the Treaty of Wallingford, sealed at Westminster in December 1153, which made Henry Stephen's heir.

THE RAZING OF LEICESTER

However, Robert's son, Robert Blanchemains, 3rd Earl of Leicester, wasn't so supportive of the new king – an action that was to have dire consequences for him and for Leicester.

In 1173, Robert sided with the king's rebellious wife, Eleanor, and her sons. The rebellion did not work out well. At the Battle of Bury St Edmunds, Robert was captured. The king's forces entered Leicestershire to seize Blanchemains's lands. Earl Shilton Castle was destroyed. But worse still lay ahead for Leicester.

On 28 July, the Siege of Leicester began. The Norman forces in the castle forced the Saxon townsfolk to hold off the king's forces. But eventually the attackers broke through and showed no mercy to the beleaguered townsfolk.

According to Throsby's history, Leicester was 'fired in several places at once and what the flames could not destroy was thrown down by force of men and engines. The Roman walls were pulled down and the town laid waste to; dismantled to wear the badge of its owner's disobedience and treason.'

While this comprehensive destruction was ongoing, Leicester Castle continued to hold out, but was eventually forced to yield. When it did, Leicester's punishment was completed. Some of the townsfolk were fined for their enforced resistance, while others were banished from the remains of their town.

THE WAR OF THE ROSES

On 22 August 1485, the forces of Richard III finally met with those of Henry Tudor at Market Bosworth.

The king had spent the night before the battle – 20 August – in Leicester's White Boar Inn, before riding out for what was to be his final battle – and the final battle of any anointed British monarch on English soil. The inn was forced to quickly change its name a few days later as the white boar was also Richard's emblem. Instead, it became the Blue Boar Inn, after the symbol of the Earl of Oxford, one of the new king's allies.

Richard had the dominant army until the troops of Sir William Stanley – who had sworn allegiance to Richard despite being Henry Tudor's stepfather – deserted the king.

According to local accounts, villagers at Stoke Golding climbed the battlements of St Margaret of Antioch church to watch the battle. Grooves in the windowsills of the church are attributed to soldiers sharpening their swords there on the battle's eve.

Stoke Golding was also to play another part in the end of the War of the Roses – and the beginning of the new regime, for the village played host to the crowning of the new king and was thus the 'birthplace of the Tudor dynasty'. After the battle, Henry and his entourage retired to the hilly country near the village. The coronation was performed with a 'circlet' (possibly Richard's) retrieved from a thorn bush. The crowning itself occurred in the area now known as Crown Hill and Crown Hill Field.

In the meantime, large pits were dug around the villages of neighbouring Dadlington and Fenny Drayton where the battlefield dead were buried. Richard's body was returned to Leicester. Henry Tudor had the body displayed ignominiously for a number of days, and then ordered that it be buried in the nearby Franciscan Abbey (Greyfriars), which stood close to St Martin's church, now the Cathedral.

Debates revolved about the exact location of the battlefield. Ambion Hill was the favoured location and is the site of the battlefield heritage centre, due to a sentence in the chronicles of Raphael Holinshed, who wrote in 1577 that Richard, the night before the battle 'pitched his field on a hill called Anne Beame, refreshed his soldiers and took his rest'. This was interpreted to mean that Ambion Hill was the battlefield site. But there were other local contenders.

Between 2005 and 2009, a large-scale project by Glenn Foard of the Battlefield Trust attempted to identify a definitive location. The core area of the battlefield has now been established at Fenn Lane, 2 miles south-west of the visitor centre. The decisive evidence was a concentration of cannonball and gun shot, remains of an ancient marsh – which corresponds with the mire where Richard's horse was lost – and a small silver gilt badge shaped like a boar – the emblem of Richard III – which was given out to his followers.

Ambion Hill, however, still remains part of the wider battlefield.

REFORMATION RISINGS

The advent of the Tudor dynasty did no more to ensure peace in Leicestershire than any of the previous regimes. All was quiet through the reign of Henry VIII but with his death, and the death of his most immediate heir, the boy king Edward, disruption once again broke out.

Leicestershire was central to much of this, not least because Lady Jane Grey, the nine days queen who briefly supplanted the rightful Queen Mary, was a local girl.

Leicestershire formally declared allegiance to Mary instead, but that did not stop the county harbouring pockets of unrest.

WYATT'S REBELLION

Learning no lessons from his daughter's historically short reign and imprisonment at the hands of her disgruntled cousin, Jane's father, Henry Grey, 1st Duke of Suffolk, decided to have another pop at his rightful monarch – along with his brother Thomas, the Earl of Devon, and various other peeved peers.

The lords of the rebellion, known as Wyatt's Rebellion, were supposed to raise support from their counties before converging on London and again replacing the queen – this time with her sister Elizabeth. However, the rebellion was thwarted when the Crown got wind of it.

Some of the would-be rebels had the sense to withdraw but Henry Grey was determined to press on – but he only managed to raise

140 men. He finally gave himself up but was tried and beheaded, with his daughter and his son-in-law following him. The irony is that if Grey had not revolted, Jane would probably have lived, as Mary well knew she was only a pawn. Wyatt's Rebellion, however, convinced her that she could remain a nucleus for dissent – unless she was removed from the board of play.

Meanwhile, Leicester itself was the scene of local repercussions when John Kettle, who seems to have been part of the rebellion, was hung, drawn and quartered in the town on 9 March 1554 – the only such execution in the town's history.

Kettle's remains – according to the town accounts – were displayed about Leicester; his head fitted to the High Cross and his four quarters over the town gates.

MAY DAY AND PURITANS

On 1 May 1603, the town of Leicester erupted into violence when its puritan overlords attempted to suppress the traditional May Day revels.

Henry Hastings, the Earl of Huntingdon, was overlord of Leicester and a zealous puritan determined to convert the townsfolk by allowing equally enthusiastic preachers to lecture them on the error of their ways.

It did little good. The mayor of Leicester grumbled that, despite prohibitions, the townsfolk had been stealing wood from Sir Henry's estates for the idolatrous purpose of making maypoles.

So, the authorities moved in to suppress the celebrations. But the town stewards met staunch opposition and a riot ensued. The people of Leicester roamed the streets, many armed with guns, seeking out the puritan killjoys. Things didn't settle down for another two weeks.

THE MIDLAND REVOLT

The Midland Revolt was a series of riots that arose in the Midlands as a protest against the enclosure of common land. It was led by a tinker called John Reynolds, otherwise known as Captain Pouch because he promised his supporters by 'the contents of his pouch' that they would suffer no harm by defying the authorities.

The intention of the revolt was to destroy the enclosures, but Pouch urged his followers not to use violence in their endeavours. Instead, the idea was to tear down the hedges and fences enclosing the land.

The revolt began in the spring of 1607 in Northamptonshire and by May had spread to Leicestershire. Five thousand people massed at Cotesbach in Leicestershire, where the owner of the land, John Quarles, had raised the rent for his tenant farmers – no doubt to drive them out so that he could add their farms to the other parcels of land that he had already begun to enclose for sheep farming.

To stem the flow of supporters for the Cotesbach protest, a curfew was imposed upon Leicester and a gibbet raised to warn the people of the consequences of the riot. It did little good, as the townsfolk simply tore it down.

But the revolt was also as ineffectual, for by 1612 the enclosure of land was complete and never repealed.

THE ENGLISH CIVIL WAR

With very few exceptions, Leicestershire was firmly on the side of Parliament during the English Civil War. Although Viscount Falkland of Shilton Park, Tooley, backed the king (and died for it), other great families were against the Crown.

Unsurprisingly, the Greys of Groby took the side of the rebels – probably because of their past tussles with the Crown. But the clergy was also on the side of Parliament and were often targets for vengeful Crown loyalists. In March 1644, Colonel Hastings of Ashby de la Zouch led four troops of horses around the county, arresting 100 clergymen and their supporters. They were held at Hinckley church.

Leicester was firmly in Parliament's camp and on 30 May 1645, Royalist forces laid siege to the town, breaching the walls in the early hours of the morning of the 31st.

The Royalist's retribution on the town was merciless. While defenders on the town's rooftops attempted to drive them off with shot and roof tiles, the royalist forces drove Leicester's forces further into the centre of Leicester until they were forced to make a last stand at High Cross and St Martin's churchyard. Here, the townspeople finally laid down their weapons – only to be charged by the Royalist cavalry.

At the trial of Charles I, it was claimed the king himself egged his troops on. A Humphrey Brown testified that Charles was heard to say, 'I do not care if they are cut, they are mine enemies.'

Whether Charles gave the order or not, the Royalist repercussions were bloody. Women and children were dragged from their homes and killed, and members of the town committee were hanged or dismembered. By the end of the siege, 709 people were estimated to be dead.

A month later, in June 1645, Market Harborough became the headquarters of the king's army. It was while in the town that Charles I decided to confront Parliamentary forces at nearby Naseby, just over the border in Northamptonshire. The Battle of Naseby proved a decisive victory for Parliament led by Oliver Cromwell, and, after the battle, Harborough chapel became a temporary prison for the captured forces.

Following the battle, Parliamentary forces pursued the defeated Royalists over the border into Leicestershire and Great Glen. Here the church was vandalised during the ensuing skirmish and still bears the scars today. Modern Great Glen preserves its memories of the episode in five road names: Cromwell Road, Naseby Way, Rupert's Way, Edgehill Close and Halford Close.

Both sides were guilty of putting the people of Leicestershire to great hardship through looting. In 1642, Parliamentary troops stole horses and provisions from villages near Ashby Parva, and in 1646, the citizens of Dadlington lodged a complaint with the Warwickshire County Committee that on 12 March 1643, a Parliamentary soldier called Burdett made off with a horse belonging to a local widow.

TWENTIETH-CENTURY CONFLICT

THE FIRST WORLD WAR

Zeppelins over Loughborough

On 31 January 1916, nine Zeppelin airships set out to bomb Liverpool docks but missed their target because of fog. Blackout was not mandatory during the First World War, especially in many country towns, so it was easy for the airships to spot the lights of Loughborough. Having done so, the commander, Captain Franz Stabert, gave the order to drop the bombs over there instead.

Bombs landed in Ashby Square, The Rushes and Thomas Street, with the fourth and final bomb killing five people on Empress Road. In all, ten people died during the raid. The airship went on to drop bombs on Ilkeston and Burton upon Trent.

The Great Donington Escape

During the war, Donington Hall in Castle Donington served as a prisoner-of-war camp with two 6ft-high electric barbed-wire fences and an electric wire around its perimeter.

Yet despite these precautions, in the summer of 1915 Gunther Plüschow successfully escaped not only Donington but Britain – the only German PoW to do so in two world wars. Plüschow recalled in his memoirs how:

> Day and night I planned, brooded, deliberated how I could escape from this miserable imprisonment ... I had to act with the greatest calm and caution if I hoped to succeed.

After quizzing a guard and discovering the nearest train station was at Derby, Plüschow obtained civilian clothes and hid with another inmate while the other prisoners deceived the nightly roll call. At 12.30 a.m., using a ladder and planks to scale the fence, the two men escaped.

Making their way cross-country to Derby, the pair split up and made for London via Leicester. Although his companion was captured, Plüschow's English was better and helped him convince people he was an American seaman. An attempt was even made to recruit him to the British army!

At Gravesend, Plüschow stole a rowing boat and stowed away on the SS *Princess Juliana* and so reached Europe, earning himself the Iron Cross for his successful escape a few weeks later.

Leicestershire's 'Thankful Villages'

'Thankful' or 'blessed' villages were so named because all of the men they sent off to the First World War returned home alive. Some fifty-three villages across England and Wales figure in their number. Leicestershire has five: Saxby, East Norton, Stretton en le Field, Willesley and Willoughby Waterleys.

No war memorials exist in these villages, but their churches do bear plaques to celebrate those who fought and returned home alive.

The Carillon Tower

By the end of the First World War, Loughborough had lost 400 men and a unique monument was built in the town's Queen's Park: a bell tower. Loughborough's carillon is made up of forty-seven bells of differing sizes. The range of bells allows for a diverse range of musical notes, thus allowing bell ringers to play a variety of tunes on an instrument similar to an organ but consisting of levers.

Donors had their names inscribed on the bells. One was Edmund Denis Taylor, the head of Taylor's bell foundry that forged the bells – and uncle of three of the lost.

THE SECOND WORLD WAR

Leicestershire Blitzes

Leicester survived the war with relatively few major bombings. But on 19 November 1940, the city was attacked by enemy aircraft from 7.45 in the evening until the early hours of the following morning.

The worst of the bombing centred on the Highfields district of the city, where forty people were killed. Buses were brought out in the blackout to evacuate residents, while others sought sanctuary on the open ground of Victoria Park. In those few hours, over 150 high-explosive bombs were dropped on the city, killing 108 people, injuring 284 and destroying 255 homes and fifty-six industrial premises.

The rest of the county suffered equally. In 1941, Kirby Muxloe was heavily bombed when a German bomber returning from a raid on Coventry emptied its load on two streets, destroying the Free Church and several houses. Gaps left in the houses can still be seen today.

Earl Shilton was also targeted, having 192 air-raid alerts during the war, the first on 26 June 1940, the last on 20 March 1945. During one of those raids in November 1940, two parachute mines landed on the village. One mine failed to explode and there were no casualties.

The most frightening attack on the village occurred at 7 a.m. on 27 July 1942 when a lone German bomber attacked, dropping three stick bombs. Farm buildings were badly damaged and a bull so badly injured it had to be destroyed.

But it could have been much worse. Mr T.J. Langton, then an Earl Shilton schoolboy, recalls how:

> On this particular morning a lost German plane flew low over Keats Lane and ... this plane flew over low and sprayed machine gun bullets along Keats Lane. He ran into an entry and dropped his scarf. When he eventually recovered it, he noticed it contained a bullet hole. He told the story to Michael Mortimore, the son of the village bobby who also attended the school. On hearing this, Mike Mortimore said it was a good job he had not got it wrapped round his neck, at the time.

Barwell's Unexploded Bomb
Other bombs that fell didn't explode – well, not immediately. Barwell was one such place where the army dealt with the device. Around a 1-mile radius was cleared and locals were told to stay indoors while the experts did their work.

The army bomb disposal expert approached the bomb dressed for a speedy exit – in shorts and running shoes. But his careful detonation of the bomb had to be halted when learner fliers from the local Desford airbase took to the skies above, leading to a delay in the detonation.

Once the planes were clear it was back to work on the bomb. But setting it off it was by no means smooth. Although no one was hurt, the nose of the bomb ended up in a greenhouse in nearby Elmesthorpe – a distance of just under 2 miles away!

HEROES AND HEROINES

Many Leicestershire folk have played their parts – big and small – in war and conflict. Here are just a few.

Richard Henry Burton (1923–93) was awarded the Victoria Cross in the Second World War. Born in Melton Mowbray, Burton was a 21-year-old private when he took the lead in an attack near Florence, taking out enemy machine-gunners single-handedly so that his platoon could move forward. He also continued to act with 'magnificent gallantry and total disregard of his own safety' later in the attack, despite many of his platoon being dead or wounded.

Eliane Sophie Plewman (*née* Browne Bartroli) was born in 1917 to a Spanish mother and an English father. Eliane was educated in England and Spain, and after college moved to Leicester to work for an import company. In 1942 she began to work for the Ministry of Information, and later that year married Thomas Plewman, a royal artillery officer from Lutterworth. The couple set up home at 14 Queen's Gate Terrace, Leicester. It was through her husband that Eliane heard that Special Operations were looking for a young French-speaking woman to go undercover in France as part of a sabotage operation.

Eliane volunteered and was recruited. In 1943, she was dropped into German-occupied France. There, she assumed the identity of Madame Prunier, a Marseilles housewife, while surreptitiously providing the communications link between groups of saboteurs and intelligence-gathering agents.

On one occasion a German officer chanced to ask her for a light. Eliane had two boxes in her pocket: one of matches, the other containing a secret message she was delivering. She had no choice but to trust to blind luck and hand over one of the boxes – fortunately, it was the one without the message.

Eventually her luck ran out when her cell was betrayed by a Gestapo agent who had infiltrated their circle. On 13 September 1944, Eliane Plewman and three other SOE agents were shot at Dachau concentration camp. After the war, she was posthumously awarded the Croix de Guerre and the King's Commendation for Bravery.

OTHER HEROES

Barrow upon Soar is the birthplace of Air Vice Marshal **Johnnie Johnson**, who led many skirmishes in the Second World War and Korean War.

Born in Leicester in 1900, **Sydney (Syd) Lucas** was the last soldier to serve in both world wars. Sydney joined up just three months before the end of the conflict in 1918 and was still in training when the war ended.

Ten years later Syd and his wife emigrated to Australia, where he signed up again, this time with Australia's machine gun battalion.

This time Syd saw action. He was deployed to Palestine, but an attack of appendicitis meant he was returned to Australia and assigned to guard Italian and German PoWs. He was discharged from the army due to ill health and found work in an aircraft factory.

He died in 2008 at his home in Melbourne, Australia, at the age of 108.

But not all heroes were human. In 1914, a horse called **Songster** was drafted into the Leicestershire Yeomanry. He was assigned to trooper Bert Main of Loughborough and together they were sent to France at the start of the war.

Over eight million horses and mules died in the conflict. But Songster came back. He became a local celebrity and was cared for by Sergeant Major Harry Poole on his farm in Woodhouse Eaves. Remarkably, he lived until 1940, when he died at the age of 40, to be buried with his medal ribbons on the farm that was his last home.

TERRORISM

Leicester has twice been the target of terrorists in the twentieth century. The first time was just before the outbreak of the Second World War. The IRA, taking advantage of the unsettled situation, were upping their attacks on the mainland. In June 1939, one of their operatives constructed and posted thirteen parcel bombs, designed to go off on a train to London.

The plan, if it had come off, would have caused a major disaster. Fortunately, it never made it that far. Instead, five of the bombs went off accidentally in the Campbell Street sorting office. A postman received injuries to his hands and face but avoided serious harm. The rest of the bombs were quickly traced by the similar handwriting – and their fake London addresses – and disarmed by immersion in buckets of water.

The IRA struck again in 1990 – this time with a bomb attack on an army van parked on Rutland Street. But as in 1939, the attack was thwarted. The bomb fell off the back of the vehicle, exploding and shaking buildings within a 200-yard radius but claiming no fatalities. However, two army personnel and a civilian were treated for minor injuries.

ILLUSTRATION CREDITS

Andrews, William, *Bygone Leicestershire* (F. Murray, 1892)

Aubrey, William Hickman Smith, *The National and Domestic History of England ... With numerous steel plates, coloured pictures, etc.* (James Hagger: London, 1867)

Baldwin, Louisa, *The Shadow on the Blind and Other Ghost Stories* (J.M. Dent & Co.: London, 1895)

Brayley, E.W., *The graphic and historical illustrator; an original miscellany of literary, antiquarian, and topographical information embellished with one hundred and fifty woodcuts* (Chidley: London, 1834)

Cattermole, R., *The Great Civil War of Charles I and the Parliament* (Fisher, Son & Co.: London, 1846)

Cunningham, Henry S., *Lectures on the physiological laws of life, hygiene, and a general outline of diseases peculiar to females* (G.F. Borst & Co.: Indianapolis, 1882)

Hoffman, Professor, *Modern Magic: A Practical Treatise on the Art of Conjuring* (Routledge: London, 1885)

Hood, Thomas, *The Haunted House* (Lawrence and Bullen: London, 1896)

Independent Order of Odd Fellows, Patriarchs, Militant Drill Regulations and Ceremonies (The Friedenwald Co.: Baltimore, 1898)

Ingoldsby, Thomas, *The Ingoldsby Legends* (E.P. Dutton & Co., 1907)

Jackson, William, *The New and Complete Newgate Calendar* (Gale Ecco, 2012)

Kendall, H.B., *The Origin and History of the Primitive Methodist Church* (Dalton: London, 1880)

Loudon, J.C., *An Encyclopaedia of Agriculture* (Longman: London, 1831)

Loudon, J.C., *Trees and shrubs: an abridgment of the Arboretum et fruticetum britannicum: containing the hardy trees and schrubs of Britain, native and foreign, scientifically and popularly described: with their propagation, culture and uses and engravings of nearly all the species* (F. Warne & Co.: London, 1875)

Loudon, J.C., *An encyclopædia of gardening; comprising the theory and practice of horticulture, floriculture, arboriculture, and landscape-gardening, including all the latest improvements; a general history of gardening in all countries; and a statistical view of its present state, with suggestions for its future progress, in the British Isles* (Longman: London, 1827)

Macaulay, T.B., *The Lays of Ancient Rome* (Longman: London, 1904)

Owen, Richard, *A History of British Fossil Reptiles Vol. II* (Cassell and Company, 1849)

Pennell-Elmhirst, Edward, *The cream of Leicestershire: eleven seasons' skimmings, notable runs and incidents of the chase, selected and republished from 'The Field'* (Routledge: London, 1883)

Savage, Charles C., *Illustrated biography; or, Memoirs of the great and the good of all nations and all times; comprising sketches of eminent statesmen, philosophers, heroes, artists, reformers, philanthropists, mechanics, navigators, authors, poets, divines, soldiers, savans, etc.* (Phinney & Co.: Buffalo, 1856)

Shirley, Evelyn Philip, *Some account of English deer parks, with notes on the management of deer* (J. Murray, London, 1867)

Traill, H.D., *Social England: a record of the progress of the people in religion, laws, learning, arts, industry, commerce, science, literature and manners, from the earliest times to the present day* (Putnam: New York, 1901)

Unknown, *Library of the World's Best Literature, Ancient and modern* (University of California Libraries, 1896)

Winter, William, *'Gray Days and Gold ... New edition, revised, with illustrations'* (Macmillan and Co.: New York, 1896)

Youmans, E.L., *The Handbook of Household Science* (D. Appleton & Co.: New York, 1860)

BIBLIOGRAPHY

BOOKS AND DOCUMENTS

Bailey, Brian, *The Luddite Rebellion* (Sutton, 1998)

Betham, William, *The Baronetage of England, Or the History of the English Baronets, Volume 4* (1801)

Bevan, Jane, 'Agricultural change and the development of foxhunting in the eighteenth century', *The Agricultural History Review*, Vol. 58, No. 1, pp. 49–75 (2010)

Billson, Charles James, *County Folklore of Leicestershire and Rutland* (Brownell Press, 2013)

Billson, Charles James, *Mediaeval Leicester* (Edgar Backus: Leicester, 1920)

Breeze, Andrew 'Legionum Urbs and the British Martyrs Aaron and Julius'.(*Voprosy onomastiki.* 13 (1). pp. 30–42, 2016)

Brownlow, J.E., *The Melton Mowbray Pork Pie Industry* (University of Leicester PDF)

Cannon, J. (ed.) *The Oxford Companion to British History* (Oxford University Press, 2002)

Cantor, Leonard, *The Scheduled Ancient Monuments of Leicestershire and Rutland* (Kairos Press, Newtown Linford, 2003)

Carney, J.N., *Guide to the Geology of Bradgate Park and Swithland Wood, Charnwood Forest, BGS Occasional Report: OR/10/041* (British Geological Survey)

Carroll, Kevin K., 'The Date of Boudicca's Revolt' (Britannia, Vol. 10, 1979)

Cave, E., *The Gentleman's Magazine and Historical Chronicle, Volume 84, Part 1* (1814)

Chinnery, G.A. (ed.) *Records of the Borough of Leicester Vol. V: Hall Books and Papers 1689–1835)* (Leicester University Press, 1965)

Clay, Patrick, *The Neolithic and Bronze Age of Leicestershire and Rutland* (Transactions of the Leicestershire Archaeological and Historical Society, 73, 1999)

Copy of extract of information laid against Jane Clark of Wigston Magna and Joseph and Mary, her son and daughter in the case of witchcraft, held at the Leicester Assizes, August 1717 (County Record Office)

Courtney, Paul, *The Monastic Granges of Leicestershire* (PDF, University of Leicester)

Crawford, Elizabeth, *The Suffragette Movement* (Routledge, 1999)

Crompton, James, *Leicestershire Lollards* (Leicestershire University Library)

Curtis, John, *Topographical History of the County of Leicester* (1831)

Dryden, Alice, *Memorials of Old Leicestershire* (1911)

Fisher, Pamela, J., *Victoria County History of Leicestershire: Buckminster and Sewstern*. London: Institute of Historical Research (University of London, 2017)

Foard, Glenn, *Bosworth Battlefield: A Reassessment* (Leicestershire County Council, 2004)

Foard, Glenn and Curry, Anne, *Bosworth 1485: A Battlefield Rediscovered* (Oxford, Oxbow Books, 2013)

Hawkes, S.C., *A Late Roman Buckle from Tripontium*, (Transactions of the Birmingham and Warwickshire Archaeological Society, 1972, Vol. 85, pp. 144–159)

Henry of Knighton, *Knighton's Chronicle 1337–1396* (edited and translated by G.H. Martin, Clarendon Press: Oxford)

Hoskins, W.G., *The Anglian and Scandinavian Settlement of Leicestershire* (Anon, 1935)

Jones, D., *Loughborough: A History and Celebration* (The Francis Frith Collection, 2005)

Leicestershire Guild of Storytellers, *Leicestershire and Rutland Folk Tales* (The History Press, 2013)

Martin, R.E., *The Legends, Folklore and Dialect of Leicestershire with an Introduction on the General History of the County*

McWhirr, Alan *The Roman Swithland Slate Industry* (Leicestershire Archaeological & Historical Society)

Millward, Roy, *A History of Leicestershire and Rutland* (Phillimore, 1985)

Newitt, Ned, *The Slums of Leicester* (JMD Media Ltd, 2013)

Nichols, John, *The History and Antiquities of the County of Leicester* (1807)

Owen, C., *The Leicestershire and South Derbyshire Coalfield 1200–1900* (Ashbourne: Moorland, 1984)

Palmer, Roy, *The Folklore of Leicestershire and Rutland* (Sycamore Press, 1985)

Patterson, Temple A., *Radical Leicester* (Leicester University Press, 1954)

Powell, T.G.E., 'Late Bronze Age Hoard from Welby' (*The Archaeological Journal*, Vol. 105, Issue 1, 1948)

Pen Lloyd, Col, *The History of the Mysterious Papillon Hall* (Leicestershire Local History Council)

Phillips, Tom, *Leicestershire Folk Tales for Children* (The History Press, 2018)

Randall, J.L., *A History of the Meynell Hounds and Country, 1780–1901* (Nabu Press, 2010)

Ruddock, Elizabeth, *May Day Songs and Celebrations in Leicestershire and Rutland* (University of Leicester PDF)

Sheldon, Natasha, *Not a Guide to Leicester* (The History Press, 2013)

Sheldon, Natasha, *Leicester in 100 Dates* (The History Press, 2014)

Skinner, Julia, *Leicestershire and Rutland Recipes* (Francis Frith Collection, 2012)

Smith, Julia, *Leicester and Rutland Miscellany* (Identity Books, 2012)

Smith, Pete, *Leicester Castle, Leicester, Leicestershire: The Courtrooms in the Former Great Hall.* (Historic Buildings Report No. 19-2009, English Heritage)

Specification of Thomas Crick AD 1853, No. 542 (County Record Office)

Squires, Anthony and Jeeves, Michael, *Leicestershire and Rutland Woodlands Past and Present.* (Kairos Press, 1994)

Stevenson, Joan and Squires, Anthony, *Bradgate Park: The Childhood Home of lady Jane Grey* (Kairos Press, 1999)

Stones, E., *The Folvilles of Ashby Folville, Leicestershire, and their associates in crime, 1326–1347.* (Transactions of the Royal Historical Society 77, 1956)

Thompson, James, *The History of Leicester: From the Time of the Romans to the End of the Seventeenth Century* (J.S.C. Rossley, 1849)

Thompson, James, *The History of the Borough of Leicester in the Eighteenth Century* (Crossley and Clarke, 1871)

Thompson, James, *The Handbook of Leicester* (Thompson & Son, 1844)

Tomlin, R.S.O., *Non Coritani Sed Corieltauvi* (*The Antiquaries Journal*, 1983, Vol. LXIII, Part II, pp. 353–362)

Watts, Victor et al., *The Cambridge Dictionary of Place-Names* (Cambridge University Press, Cambridge, 2004)

Westwood, Jennifer, *Albion: A Legendary Guide to Britain* (Granada Publishing Ltd, 1985)

Westwood, Jennifer, *Haunted England: The Penguin Book of Ghosts* (Penguin, 2013)

The Woodland Trust, *The Big Picture of Woods and Trees in the UK* (PDF)

Wright, Andrew James, *Haunted Leicestershire* (Tempus Publishing, 2005)

Wright, Andrew James, *Ghosts and Hauntings In and Around Leicestershire* (Heart of Albion Press, 2006)

NEWSPAPERS AND JOURNALS

The Hinckley Times

Leicester Evening Mail

Leicester Illustrated Chronicle, 1856–1979

Leicester Mercury, 1874–

Leicester and Nottingham Journal

Melton Times

Leicester Daily Post

Leicester Guardian

Leicester Journal

Leicester Mail

Leicester Pioneer

The Telegraph

WEBSITES

Abolition:
www.bbc.co.uk/leicester/content/articles/2007/03/20/temple_and_trade_feature.shtml

Alice Hawkins: www.storyofleicester.info/city-stories/alice-hawkins

Barrow upon Soar Heritage Group:
www.barrowuponsoarheritage.org.uk/articles/village-history/local-history/the-plesiosaur.html

Belvoir Castle
'Afternoon Tea at Belvoir Castle': www.belvoircastle.com/plan-your-visit/afternoon-tea-at-belvoir-castle

The Blue Boar Inn:
www.storyofleicester.info/leisure-entertainment/the-blue-boar-inn

British County Flags:
https://britishcountyflags.com/2017/10/19/a-flag-for-leicestershire/?fbclid=IwAR3CZPQSbjZgJ9fkzVq0pfgNi6WhUX5w7VMeW8d1l8MPuBQMHKXYr2MEnCk

British History Online: www.british-history.ac.uk

British Museum:
www.britishmuseum.org/research/research_projects/all_current_
projects/the_east_leicestershire_hoards.aspx

Capital Punishment UK: www.capitalpunishmentuk.org

Centre on Dynamics of Ethnicity:
www.ethnicity.ac.uk/medialibrary/briefings/localdynamicsofdiversity/
ethnic-and-religious-mixing-in-leicestershire.pdf

Charnwood Council:
www.charnwood.gov.uk/listed_buildings/hill_fort_enclosure_
and_linear_boundary_beacon_hill_woodhouse

Duncan Lucas Collection of 'Strange Happenings in Wigston':
www.wigstonhistoricalsociety.co.uk/Strange%20
Happenings%20in%20Wigston.pdf

Encyclopaedia Britannica: www.britannica.com

Fossils UK: ukfossils.co.uk/2003/11/07/ketton-quarry

Grace's Guide to British Industrial History:
www.gracesguide.co.uk/Herbert_Morris_and_Bastert

Heraldry of the World:
www.ngw.nl/heraldrywiki/index.php?title=Leicestershire

Heritage Gateway: www.heritagegateway.org.uk/

Historic England:
Ambion: https://historicengland.org.uk/listing/the-list/list-
entry/1008549

Battle of Bosworth:
https://historicengland.org.uk/listing/the-list/list-entry/1000004

Historic UK:
www.historic-uk.com/CultureUK/Fox-Hunting-in-Britain

History of Red Leicester:
https://web.archive.org/web/20160318205929/http://www.
britishcheese.com/redleicester/history_of_red_leicester-38

Information on the River Soar and surrounding area:
http://silebymarine.co.uk/riversoar.php

Dr John Charles Bucknill (Leicester Lit & Phil Society):
www.leicesterlitandphil.org.uk/1867-john-buck-mrcs-1867-68

Leicester City Council: www.Leicester.gov.uk

Leicester City Football Club: www.lcfc.com/club/history

Leicester Mercury: www.leicestermercury.co.uk

13 Places for Spectacular Views in Leicestershire:
www.leicestermercury.co.uk/news/local-news/12-places-
spectacular-views-leicestershire-3079172

Leicestershire Apples:
www.habitat21.co.uk/leicestershire-apples-2.html

Leicestershire County Council: www.leics.gov.uk

Leicestershire County Cricket Club:
www.leicestershireccc.co.uk/lccc-history.html

Leicestershire County Parks:
www.leicscountryparks.org.uk/jubilee-woods

Leicestershire Heritage Apple Project:
www.suttonelms.org.uk/apple74.html

Leicestershire Orchard Information:
www.englandinparticular.info/orchards/o-leics-i.html

Leicestershire Police:
www.leics.police.uk/about-us/our-history/180-years

Leicestershire and Rutland Wildlife Trust: lrwt.org.uk

The Leicestershire and South Derbyshire Coal Field:
www.nmrs.org.uk/mines-map/coal-mining-in-the-british-isles/
leicestershire

Leicestershire Statistics and Research:
www.lsr-online.org/leicestershire.html

Leicestershire Villages Oral Histories:
www.le.ac.uk/emoha/community/leicsvillages.html

Local Government Association:
https://lginform.local.gov.uk/reports/lgastandard?mod-metric
=232&mod-area=E10000018&mod-group=AllCountiesIn
Country_England&mod-type=namedComparisonGroup

Mountsorrel Quarry: www.tarmac.com/mountsorrel-quarry/about

National Forest: www.nationalforest.org/forest

Natural England:
https://designatedsites.naturalengland.org.uk/SiteList.aspx?siteName
=&countyCode=26&responsiblePerson=&DesignationType=SSSI

NERC Open Research Archive: http://nora.nerc.ac.uk/8675

Ordnance Survey:
www.ordnancesurvey.co.uk/blog/2014/08/where-is-the-centre-of-
great-britain-2

Outlaws and Highwaymen: www.outlawsandhighwaymen.com

Paranormal Database:
www.paranormaldatabase.com/leicestershire/leicdata.php

Parliament UK: www.parliament.uk/about/living-

Prison Voices: www.prisonvoices.org/?p=3522

Real Crime: www.real-crime.co.uk

Rugby Archaeological Society: www.rugbyarchaeology.org.uk

Shepshed: www.shepshed.org/History.htm

The Stilton Cheese Story:
www.stiltoncheese.co.uk/the-stilton-story

Swannington Heritage:
www.swannington-heritage.co.uk/swannington_village_history.html

University of Leicester: www.le.ac.uk

The Woodland Trust: www.woodlandtrust.org.uk

The History of the Workhouse (Peter Higginbotham):
www.workhouses.org.uk

World Boxing Association:
www.wbaboxing.com/boxing-news/boxing-history-cribb-vs-
molineaux#.XbVntKecau4